# Helping Kids DEAL With Conflict

An Everyday Resource for all Teachers and Parents

## GERRY SHEANH

# PEGUIS
## PUBLISHERS

WINNIPEG • MANITOBA • CANADA

© 1996 by Gerry Sheanh

96  97  98  99  00  5  4  3  2  1

**Canadian Cataloguing in Publication Data**

Sheanh, William Gerald, 1951-
   Helping kids deal with conflict

ISBN 1-895411-79-3

1. Interpersonal conflict in children. 2. Child rearing. I. Title.

BF723.I646S48 1996    649'.1    C95-920929-8

**Editor's note**:

One of the dilemmas facing today's editor is that of retaining clarity while ensuring gender balance. This relates specifically to the use of the personal pronouns he/she, him/her, himself/herself, and so on. Using both forms in all cases makes for particularly awkward reading. In this book we have chosen to use masculine pronouns in reference to both teachers and students. We assure the reader that no affront is intended in any way.

Cover design:  Bill Stewart

Book design:  Desktop Computer Works Ltd.

Printed and bound in Canada by Hignell Printing

**Peguis Publishers**
100-318 McDermot Avenue
Winnipeg, Manitoba
Canada  R3A 0A2
1-800-667-9673

*Dedicated to the memory of my brother*
*James Stephen Sheanh*
*1958–1982*
*A born mediator who knew*
*most of these things*
*instinctively*

# Contents

# Foreword

Once upon a time the ideal family was one supported by the ideal breadwinner and cared for by the ideal mother. They reared many ideal children, and protected one another from evil outside influences. The ideal family was religious, hardworking, trustworthy, and respected and children were expected to live up to this reputation.

Judgments about the family came from outside. It had to live up to the community's idea of what an ideal family should be. But what of the family members? Were they happy, fulfilled, loving and caring of one another? Or were they constrained by trying to conform to the community's ideal?

The ideal family of today is *less* attuned to presenting a respectable front to the rest of the world and *more* attuned to fulfilling the needs of its members. That's among the findings of Colorado family specialist Dolores Curran who questioned more than 500 professionals who work with families around the United States. She found that the qualities that characterize the healthy family of today are "relational."

Among the family specialists Curran talked to, all agreed that the most important traits of the healthy family are "communicating and listening." Communicating means to understand and accept differences among family members and to respect others' opinions. Listening includes reading body language and hearing silence as a means of communication. Young people growing up in a family in which differences of opinion are aired, not forbidden, are less likely than others to indulge in "group think" later in life and are more likely than their peers to accept individual differences.

Curran found that the second most important traits in the healthy family are "affirming and supporting." Members of healthy, happy families like each other, and often tell each other that. Such family support gives members a sense of personal worth. They enjoy being together, which makes their relationship very satisfying. The family and its individual members can build on these affirming strengths.

Psychologist Abraham Maslow pointed out that we are the first generation in history to be sufficiently beyond fulfilling our sustenance needs to be able to focus on the quality of our relationships. That adds a new dimension to our lives—one that takes effort to accomplish.

*Helping Kids Deal with Conflict* is a thoughtful and caring look at the problems encountered by kids who suffer from too much pressure and not enough real-life relational skills. It is a thorough and understandable guide today's teachers and parents can use to help them break the log jam of conflict and begin rebuilding the warmth and support all kids should have.

Dr. Joyce Brothers
Fort Lee, New Jersey

# Acknowledgments

I have been very fortunate, during the writing of this book, to enjoy a tremendous level of support and encouragement from a number of people. To these people, I extend my sincerest appreciation and gratitude.

To Bill, Gerry, and Trevor Clare for suggesting that this book be written, for their constant encouragement, and for pointing me in the right direction.

To Judy Norget for her precise, painstaking work on the original manuscript and for her gentle guidance in clarifying my meaning.

To Doug Martin, my first editor, who began publishing my work and who encouraged me to expand my horizons.

To Paula Temrick, whose work with conflict resolution for kids inspired me to follow her example and, ultimately, to write this book.

To Clare LaMeres, whose inspiring work on self-esteem for kids greatly influenced my own thinking and practice.

And finally, to my daughters, Molly and Amy, who remind me almost daily that I most assuredly don't know it all, and to my wife, Joan, who put up with me throughout the writing of this book. She is the melody at the core of my life.

# Introduction

## So What's the Problem?

*Monday morning. It's only 10:30, but the teacher is already fumbling through her desk for her Tylenol. Since the opening bell:*

✧ *Steven called Joey a faggot, so Joey blackened his eye.*

✧ *Jasbir stormed out in tears when four girls refused to let her join their game.*

✧ *Arthur's jeans were tossed in the change room urinal, and though everyone knows who did it, no one will tell.*

✧ *Yakub begs to stay in at lunch because three boys have promised to pulverize him.*

✧ *Jill scrawled "I'm stupid" all over her incomplete math quiz.*

✧ *Tina, the withdrawn one, is away for the seventh day in three weeks.*

✧ *A pack of cigarettes falls out of Jean-Luc's coat pocket when another kid shoulder-checks him.*

✧ *Janet didn't do her homework because, she asserts, the teacher forgot to remind her to take it home.*

In less than two hours, the teacher has witnessed the anguish of too many vulnerable children struggling in an environment filled with conflict, which places staggering obstacles in the way of teaching, learning, growing, and living.

As we enter the twenty-first century, many children face overwhelming conflict with other children almost every day, a predicament that cries out for clear and decisive action on the part of the dominant adults—usually parents and teachers—in their lives. It is not nearly enough to say simply, "Well, that's just the way it is" or "You have to learn to take it" or "You'd better get them before they get you." The nature and alarming severity of conflicts among children has not-so-quietly accelerated to the point where even adults have little or no idea how to cope. If this seems like an alarmist overstatement of reality, consider the following actual horror stories:

⬧ A couple of years ago, a fourteen-year-old Calgary student was fatally knifed on the school ground. Reportedly a kid with few or no friends, he had approached a group of boys hoping to join them. The group didn't want him there, so someone knifed him. In former, less violent times, the group would probably have sent him away with a few caustic comments and, at worst, maybe a punch or a kick. This incident doesn't suggest much hope for the thousands of kids who don't fit in for whatever obscure or capricious reasons.

⬧ In Vancouver, a gang of toughs were hanging around a house party that had become too crowded for all those who wanted in. An innocent passerby made the mistake of making eye contact with one of the gang. His punishment was a beating, including several severe kicks to the head. The aggressor then dragged the semiconscious victim over to the concrete curb and laid him over it, with his backbone at right angles to the gutter. He then proceeded to jump on the victim in a mindlessly violent practice known as curbing. The aggressor was eventually caught, but the victim spent a protracted period in a coma and today is permanently brain-injured.

⬧ In Toronto, every June 1 is Skip Day, a high school student tradition. In other, more peaceful times, hordes of kids would ferry over to Centre Island to spend the day happily goofing off. On one recent Skip Day, several hundred students became embroiled in a virtual gang war, using crude weapons to maim the enemy. The melee quickly escalated when one student dared to take someone else's hat, and the battle lines were drawn.

✧ A sixteen-year-old in Surrey, B.C. got off a bus late one evening and encountered a group of three or four others. The boy had a Chicago White Sox hat on, to which he had taped a piece of chewing gum for some playful reason. One of the boys expressed offense that the hat-wearer was "dissing" the White Sox, then pulled a knife and killed him. Dissing is an urban, Black American term meaning "disrespecting," an offense that draws immediate and violent correction. Gang wars are routinely fought over someone dissing someone else.

✧ Also in Surrey, a thirteen-year-old boy was reported missing early in the school year. The police, his family, and his friends combed the area, putting up posters on bulletin boards, fences, telephone poles—anywhere they could—pleading for information. The silence was deafening. It was as though he'd disappeared from the planet.

The boy's body was eventually recovered, and in the ensuing investigation it was revealed that he'd been killed by another student whom he'd "burned" in a drug deal. The murder weapon was a large rock, and the body had been carefully hidden. It also turned out that a number of kids at school knew all about it, but no one would break the code of silence by telling the police. Sadly, the boy who finally *did* tell was harassed and threatened by other students for breaking the code. He and his family required police protection. Not much of an incentive for moral and ethical behavior.

There are scores of other examples, from the escalation of violence in schools across North America to the rash of suicides among Japanese schoolboys who find death an attractive alternative to constant bullying. Violence by minors has become a frequently publicized issue, with nearly everyone trying first to define and measure it, and then to offer varied prescriptions.

Academics, existing within the buffered world of the university campus, attempt to apply theoretical constructs and scientific methods to the issue. Some announce that violence is no more prevalent than it ever was; others insist that there is no empirical proof. Perhaps not, but ask any parent, teacher, administrator, probation official, or police officer and a dramatically different story emerges. These people grow ever more alarmed by violent kids and are far less interested in philosophical discussions than they are in finding practical solutions.

The more conservative and reactionary often advocate a strengthening of laws concerning young offenders. They place heavy emphasis on stricter enforcement and more severe punishment, believing these to be deterrents. Maybe, maybe not. But stricter enforcement and more draconian penalties would still not address the causes of the behavior, only the outcomes.

The less conservative advocate a different vision, one that attempts to be preventive instead of reactionary. This group wants to help all children who have to deal with conflict by modeling and teaching conflict resolution skills; moral and ethical behavior; how to enhance self-esteem; how to resist negative peer influence; how to effectively cope with bullying, put-downs, and teasing; how to make decisions and solve problems; and how to synthesize it all into a positive, constructive way of dealing with all kinds of people in society. This book is written from this perspective.

This book is intended to help provide a vision of the possible, a guide to helping children of all ages become emotionally stronger, more self-assured, and fully equipped to deal with those people in their lives who seem to want nothing more than to put them down, beat them down, or grind them down. It is also designed to provide teachers and parents with a number of different approaches to help not only their children, but themselves as well.

Kids much like those described at the very beginning of this introduction exist in nearly every classroom in nearly every school. By extension these are *our* children—and our children's friends and acquaintances at school. And what might their conflicts be?

◇ Steven, the kid who called another kid a faggot, is verbally aggressive, and Joey has low impulse control. Joey also forgot the first rule for dealing with bullies—if you give a bully what he wants, the bully wins—and he reacted to Steven's taunts. Sure, Steven ended up with a black eye, but he succeeded in getting Joey to take the bait. Neither understands the concept of escalation of conflict, so neither has any idea how to stop it from deteriorating into a fight.

✧ Jasbir, who stormed out in tears, is the victim of ostracism; it doesn't really matter why. She most assuredly has been made to see that she doesn't fit in. The four other girls found strength in numbers, and by issuing a group command, none felt personally responsible. That crashing sound you heard was Jasbir's self-esteem hitting the floor.

✧ Arthur, whose jeans were tossed in the urinal, is probably that child whom everyone picks on just to see him upset; they also know he's not likely to stand up for himself. The code of silence is a strong indication of the effect of peer pressure; no one will speak up for fear that *his* clothing may end up in the urinal too. Some classmates may actually feel ashamed that they didn't speak up, but they'd rather feel ashamed than become victims themselves.

✧ Yakub, who wants to stay in at lunch, is terrified by the bullies, who use threats of physical violence to maintain their reputations among their peers. They gain power by stealing it from others, thus making the others powerless.

✧ Jill, who scrawled "I'm stupid" on her math quiz, isn't really stupid, but she truly believes she is. She views her mistakes and lack of quick understanding as evidence of her own personal worthlessness. This sense of worthlessness has taken years to develop, through repeated negative messages from home and school. She has internalized a false logic: to make an error is stupid. I made a mistake; therefore I am stupid. Healthy self-esteem is completely absent.

✧ Tina, the withdrawn child, uses escapism to avoid unpleasantness. Perhaps she is ridiculed or teased, ostracized or bullied, or maybe all of these. Perhaps she suffers from physical ailments linked to emotional ill-health, stress, or unresolved conflict. What she most definitely is *not* is safe—emotionally, physically, or psychologically.

✧ Jean-Luc's cigarette package could mean a few things. His smoking could be self-destructive behavior based on shaky self-esteem; it could be an attempt to make his own decisions; or it could be a desire to achieve status within his peer group. Any way you look at it, it's a problem, since it appears to be rooted in some sort of powerlessness.

✧ Janet, who didn't do her homework, always places the blame for her misfortunes on someone else. She actually believes it was the teacher's responsibility to remind her about the homework. This blaming behavior may well be the result of her internalized belief that being wrong or making mistakes means she is dumb, stupid, bad, or any other negative state of existence. She will offer the most absurd reasons why she can't possibly be responsible. To bring her to the point where she will accept responsibility will be a difficult mission.

In the chapters that follow, each of these issues will be discussed in detail. Examples and actual stories of kids in conflict will be used, though the kids' names have been changed. Practical tips for teachers and parents will be provided as food for thought and as a sort of mirror against which we can examine our own beliefs, values, opinions, wants, needs, and behaviors.

If you have read this far, you already know (1) of the critical need to help kids, (2) that you are open to any ideas that will help you help them, and (3) that you want to help make a difference.

While you may not agree with everything in this book— and I'd be genuinely surprised if you did—there is much here that you should find helpful. I have two pieces of advice:

1. Read this book in chunks—and not necessarily from front to back—to allow yourself time for reflection and insight. You might want to read one chapter one day, another on another day.

2. Adapt what is useful to you, add it to what you already know, and then adopt it as your own. I make no claim to

knowing it all, and I hope this book is as much an impetus for change for you as it has been for me.

Nothing worthwhile was ever accomplished without extreme effort, persistence, and willingness to change focus as the images shifted. And making a real difference in a child's life might be your most important accomplishment.

I wish you luck in achieving your goal of helping children, just as I wish children everywhere the opportunity to grow and learn in a supportive, positive environment, where managing conflict is accomplished as easily as tying your shoelaces, making a sandwich, or using a television remote control. Taught and modeled—and practiced repeatedly—the ideas that follow will help you meet that goal.

# In the Jaws of the Dragon:
# The Faces of Conflict

## About Geoff

*There is a teacher I greatly admire whom I'll call Emma. I admire her for her optimism when talking about her students, and for her compassion, empathy, and clear, deliberate commitment to championing the underdog. Emma told me a story recently about Geoff, a grade-seven student in her school.*

*The school serves a low socioeconomic area with an increasing number of what have come to be termed "at-risk" families. Unemployment, alcohol abuse, domestic violence, broken families, and other serious social issues are more prevalent here than in most other areas of town.*

*Geoff comes from a home where his only resident parent (his mother) is an alcoholic. He has no brothers or sisters and, in a peculiar way, is more adult than his mother. Emma reports that Geoff is the parent, taking care of his mother and running errands for her when she is unable to focus on much else but the bottle. She will even call the school and ask for Geoff to be sent home so that he can do some chores for her. Geoff endures tremendous conflict in his home life, and it shows up at school as well. Geoff is an easy target for the taunts and teasing of his classmates, who seem to love getting him mad because he almost inevitably erupts and fights back. And when he fights, he is invariably suspended, the most recent time for five days.*

*After Geoff returned to school, Emma saw him sitting on a chair in front of the office one afternoon and asked him how he*

*was doing. He burst into tears and, in a torrent of loosely
connected statements, told her he'd got into another fight and
was going to be suspended and he just couldn't take it anymore
and he just* HATED *it here. Emma consoled him as best she
could, but mostly just listened.*

*At the end of the day, as Geoff was getting his coat to go
home, one of his classmates barged out of the classroom, saw
him, and shouted, "Hey, let's beat the shit out of Geoff." Emma
was furious, though not with the swearing—it was the least of
the problem. She was angry at the treatment that Geoff, so
obviously unhappy and emotionally fragile, had to endure daily
at the hands of his callous classmates, and she was angry at the
never-ending conflict in his everyday life.*

*So far, there's no happy ending for Geoff. He continues to
live in conflict and in fear of being bullied. Emma's heart breaks
when she talks about him, and she displays a steely-eyed
resolve when she asserts that she'll do whatever she can to look
out for him, be there when he wants to talk, and protect him if
need be. All well and good, but she's also wise enough to know
that there is little that she can do to change the multiplicity of
conditions that contribute to his conflicts. So she does what she
can—and she hopes.*

## What Creates Conflict?

We live in a world that's in perpetual conflict, and as much
as we might like to avoid or eliminate it, conflict is inevitable. Examples abound, from the schoolyard wrestling match
over some real or imagined slight, to entire nations mobiliz-
ing their resources in an attempt to crush any threat to their
national interests. In each instance, conflict has been resolved by aggression, with the disputants resigned to playing
out their roles in a pretty predictable manner. To address
alternative ways of resolving conflict, it is first necessary to
come to some agreement about what we mean when we talk
about conflict.

While there are many ways to think about and discuss it,
the following precipitating factors should help in conceptual-
izing conflict:

- ✦ **Conflict arises from competition for scarce resources.** Such resources can be material objects (like the basketball that two students fight over at lunch hour), to who gets the house after a marital breakdown, to which candidate gets the big job in a competition for promotion. Resources can also be intangible things like parents' attention, a coveted role within the peer group, or custody of the television remote control.

  Conflict occurs because everyone wants what he sees as his fair share, which is almost always more than the other person thinks he should get. Disputants employ elaborate strategies to get what they want, with the winner achieving a dual victory: (1) winning the battle and (2) having the pleasure of seeing the other person lose.

- ✦ **Conflict is the difference between what is and what is desired.** Conflict is common among adolescents, who frequently wish they were more than or better than they are, or at least better than they perceive themselves to be. "If only I were slimmer [taller, prettier, more muscular, more popular, or had unblemished skin], I'd be happier." These conflicts between the real and the ideal frequently continue into adulthood.

- ✦ **Conflict occurs when there is an imbalance of power.** Power is a huge issue, since we encounter someone or some agency that has authority or power over us every day. We naturally want to balance that power, just as those with power want nothing so much as to hoard it.

  Power imbalance is probably the number one factor in the conflict between early adolescent children and their parents, teachers, and peer-group leaders. Children who aren't given the chance to exercise some power over things that affect them, like clothing, choice of friends, choice of free-time activities, will typically attempt to level the playing field by going against the demands of the power figures in their lives. In short, kids can always punish you by *not* doing what you want them to do; it is, to them, one way of winning back some form of power.

Taken together, these three truisms about conflict help form a fundamental framework in which all kinds of issues around conflict can be examined and analyzed. One of the most important issues deals with the many phenomena that make up the contexts of conflict.

## Contexts of Conflict

The culture we live in is fragile, fragmented, and difficult to define. Conflicting values, needs, wants, beliefs, attitudes, and aspirations exist side by side, making it difficult to find an ideal we can subscribe to. This is a marked difference from the times many of us tend to look back upon with some nostalgia.

Those of us who went to school in the fifties and sixties often bemoan the fact that simple, everyday living has become so complex. In those days, the big issues in education related mostly to control of behavior and compliance with authority. The school represented a means of social control and a vehicle for the transmission of community values and expectations. Compliant behavior was usual and expected, giving rise to a number of beliefs:

◇ that the teacher and principal were almost always right

◇ that respect for authority was a condition of survival

◇ that punishment was necessary for breaches of the rules

◇ that intelligence testing was a valid means of sorting the able from the unable

◇ that kids who couldn't or wouldn't learn through conventional means of instruction should be ignored and left to find their own way

◇ that curriculum was a body of content requiring mastery through repetition and rote learning

◇ that schools were responsible for filling children's brains with skills and facts and were not responsible for what was thought to be more properly the responsibility of the parents

◇ that schools should reflect and reinforce cultural values and norms of behavior

Fast-forward to today and a very different picture emerges. Although schools still try to reflect community values, there are scores of different values systems out there. We find ourselves struggling to make sense of the overwhelming diversity of conflicting beliefs and values, often becoming more confused than ever. Where schools once conducted their affairs within the assumption of broad-based parental and community support, such support can no longer be taken for granted.

Different parents want different things from schools. Some believe in the traditional role of the schools they went to as children, while others believe that their children deserve an individually customized education. Some challenge both the content and need for certain curricula and seek to have their children exempted from having to learn them. Some want to emphasize competition within the classroom, while others demand a cooperative approach based on working together toward a common goal. Some view schooling as preparation for the job market, while others see it as personal, intellectual development. It is small wonder that teachers and administrators have difficulty reconciling such conflicting demands; there doesn't seem to be any benchmark at all.

Moreover, the conflicts within our culture tend to be largely responsible for a reactive school system that tries to meet everyone's needs. Many conflicts stem from intolerance of the beliefs and values of others, greed, and the loss of faith in our formerly solid social institutions such as the family, the church, and government. These factors lead to increasing feelings of powerlessness, hopelessness, stress, and anxiety. It is evident that rapid, complex, and overwhelming social change has left everyone scrambling to make sense of it all, and to find a comfortable niche within our culture.

Popular culture seems built on a foundation of ambiguity. Television portrayals of family life send out strange messages. Kids are almost always seen as quick-witted, wise, and funny, and quick to use verbal communications that few of us would accept from our own children. Moms may be superwomen or charming bimbos; Dads are either macho heroes or awkward and sentimental bumblers. Hardly anyone fits these exaggerated stereotypes so, in the kids' eyes, all *real* people—themselves and their parents—just don't measure up. The problem with this is that these types of characterizations tend to influence the way people—especially children—view the world. There is a substantial difference between the behavior of television characters whom kids model and what teachers and parents expect, a difference that can contribute to ongoing conflict.

Another troubling aspect of popular culture is the depiction of conflict and violence in film. Violence—particularly spectacular, bloodletting, explosive violence—sells tickets and rents videos.

The debate as to whether or not TV and film violence has a direct influence on the behavior of children continues to rage, and it is not my intent to offer a definitive answer. I do believe, however, that continuous exposure to anything over a long period of time tends to anaesthetize us. We simply get used to it, and so do kids.

It is not just the overt violence that is troubling, though. Underlying messages that sell movie tickets are potentially more damaging. Some of these themes include:

If someone hurts you, it's okay to hurt them back.

Revenge is sweetest when your opponent dies.

Revenge is justified, almost obligatory, and not subject to consequences.

It is perfectly acceptable to resist authority.

Authority figures are usually bumbling fools.

He who loses is a loser, and therefore contemptible.

So, we should not be surprised to see children mirroring these values in the schoolyard. It would be simplistic to point to films as a direct cause of violence, but it would also be foolish to dismiss them as having no influence. Just as there is no single factor that permits a flower to germinate and flourish, neither is there one single cause for conflict and violence among children.

There are other aspects of popular culture that contribute to ambiguity. Roles and expectations for certain behaviors continue to evolve, with more public discussion of women's rights, minority rights, aboriginal rights, gay rights, and so on. Each of these issues is highly emotional, with battle lines drawn everywhere, crisscrossing each other like branches on a weeping willow. It seems as though no one can figure out who or what they're supposed to be anymore, which gives rise to the kind of uncertainty that fuels conflict, both internally within each person, and externally with respect to how we relate to others. Our confidence and sense of certainty become shaken.

I have long believed that what we call happiness or satisfaction is directly related to the degree of certainty in our lives—in our relationships, our conditions of employment, our place in our families and in the community. When our feelings of certainty are threatened, we experience stress and we seek to find ways of correcting this uncomfortable feeling. In a sense, we seek to find out what the cultural norms are and to tailor our behavior accordingly. All this is fine if a cultural norm actually exists, but there doesn't seem to be one anymore. So we adopt one or more strategies for self-protection.

Almost nothing exists in isolation, certainly not conflict. Conflict is both a cause and an effect emerging from complex human interactions. Conflict can exist within an individual, between two persons, between a person and a group, and among groups. Conflict often carries with it intense emotions such as fear, anger, alienation, and anxiety. Conflict also generates a variety of coping responses, ranging from complete withdrawal to enthusiastic acceptance, and everything in between. One thing seems certain: without an understanding of the contexts in which conflict emerges, finding ways of managing it in our children's and our own everyday lives is almost impossible.

## Strategies for Self-preservation

To better understand the ambiguity of conflict, it is useful to examine four broadly defined strategies for preservation.

## Cocooning: Hide in Your Shell

This strategy consists of a form of withdrawal that futurist Faith Popcorn has termed "cocooning," the act of pulling back within the safety of the home and family. Within the cocoon, beliefs, values, and standards of behavior can be both defined and practiced without fear of outside interference. Record sales of expensive home entertainment systems, computers, hot tubs, and exercise equipment are strong evidence that more of us are retreating from the confusion of popular culture. The people who use this strategy want to take more control of their lives by controlling what they can; in other words, if it's too crazy to get by out there, we'll create a better world within our own four walls.

## Competition: Strike First, Strike Hard

Another strategy consists of adopting an aggressive, competitive stance that seeks to achieve certainty through controlling as much as we can and as many people as possible. This could be termed self-preservation through intimidation. It is anchored to a willingness to live in nearly continual conflict. The people who use this strategy become entrenched in modes of thinking and behavior that have worked for them in the past. Accompanying this entrenchment is often a sense of embitterment at the kinds of changes that are difficult, often impossible, to control. People employing this strategy can be stubborn and inflexible, though they consider themselves independent and consistent. Either way, they are masters at finding the personally expedient solution.

## Passivity: Blend with the Scenery

A third strategy is used by those people who are practically always willing to adapt themselves to any situation, having an almost chameleon-like ability to fit themselves into whatever context is necessary for personal survival. They can behave one way at home and with friends, and quite another in the outside world. They are able to freely switch between the extremes of compassion and coldness, tolerance and intolerance, optimism and pessimism, acceptance and rejection, generosity and greed, and risk taking and playing it safe. These people either have it very much together, or are so used to tailoring their behavior to meet the perceived expectations of others that they have difficulty deciding who or what they really are. Either way, they survive, but barely.

### Enthusiastic Acceptance: Just Do It

A fourth strategy is employed by people who look upon change, and the inevitable conflicts it creates, as an opportunity for growth and learning. These are the people who are quick to assess possibilities and can formulate a positive vision, along with a plan for getting there. These people are not chained to the past and are unafraid of committing errors along the way to fulfilling their goals. These people are rarer than the other three types, and generally the most successful. They are also the kind of people we should hope our kids will become.

No matter which strategy people use to keep themselves as secure as possible in a confusing world, all but the fourth strategy—enthusiastic acceptance—appear rooted in fear. Fear of the unknown consequences of change affects a great many people. Tough questions flood the mind: Will I lose my job? My home? My place in the world? My money? My reputation? My sense of certainty and security? We all fear losing whatever it is that has taken a long time to acquire. In essence, we live in fear of the systematic destruction of the world we've constructed for ourselves by forces beyond our control, and it all adds up to conflict with a capital C.

## Key Concepts Concerning Conflict

Having dealt with three ways of thinking about conflict, the contexts in which conflicts arise, and strategies for self-preservation, let's explore some of the components of conflict. The first of these deals with human response to conflict.

## Fight, Freeze, or Flee Responses

When we are attacked or threatened, it is very difficult to employ rational thought to meet the threat. The body and mind instinctively take over and begin a chain reaction that is largely unconscious.

The heart begins to beat faster, increasing blood flow, which causes flushing of the face and lightness in the limbs. Our adrenal glands send a whoosh of adrenaline into the accelerated blood flow, immediately giving us extra speed and strength. Our hands may begin to shake, probably from an excess of an as-yet-unused jolt of adrenaline. Our stomachs may do a quick flip, causing sudden nausea. What *doesn't* happen is clear, deliberative thought.

+ **The fight response.** A quick, reflex reaction is another response to conflict. Fighters are predisposed to stand and duke it out, with the clear intent of meeting a physical threat with a physical response. Children who end up at the principal's office as a result of a schoolyard fight almost always say that they didn't stop to consider the consequences; they just wanted to defend themselves. They are usually incapable of recalling the exact sequence of events, since everything happened so quickly that they didn't have time to think.

+ **The freeze response.** Freezers are the kids whose bodies may send them all sorts of adrenaline-induced cues, but they draw an absolute mental blank, literally doing nothing to defend themselves against the threat. These are the kids who end up getting pounded because they simply can't react, either physically enough or quickly enough. These are the kids who think of a response—something to say or do—well after the fact. This sounds like: "And when he said [or did] ..., I should have said [or done] ..." For whatever physiological reason, the conscious mind can't seem to process what the adrenaline-fueled instinct is so urgently telling it to do.

+ **The flee response.** Those who tend to flee use their rush of adrenaline to put as much distance as possible between themselves and the aggressor. Again, though, this reaction is rarely, if ever, a conscious one. In split-second time, the brain has assessed the threat and instructed the body to get out of there. Like the Freezers, these kids are often unable to explain their sudden, newfound ability to run. They are rarely involved in fights because they are such able escapists.

## Alternative Responses

In helping kids develop skills for resolving conflicts, the first important concept to internalize is that there *is* an alternative to the fight-freeze-flee reaction. What we want to try to accomplish is to have the student (1) recognize the situation as a threat, (2) realize that a fight, freeze, or flee reaction is common, and (3) overcome these instinctive reactions through rational assessment of the threat and employing a strategy to deal with it. Sounds really easy if you say it fast.

One technique borrowed from psychology is called positive *self-talk*. Self-talk is just that; we talk to ourselves about what is happening and what our responses might be. Consider the following scene:

> Kim is minding her own business when Marie comes up and says something provocative, such as, "I heard you've been telling everyone you could beat me up." Kim responds, "No, I didn't." This is not enough for Marie, whose intent was to beat the daylights out of Kim anyway.
>
> Without knowing about fight-freeze-flee, Kim's instincts take over and she doesn't even attempt to assess the threat rationally. She runs, and later feels ashamed because her classmates laughed at her for her cowardice.
>
> Using self-talk, Kim could achieve a different outcome. Here's how that could sound:
>
> "Marie is looking for a fight. I don't want to fight. I'd really like to get out of here, but that will only make it worse. Maybe I can talk her out of it. Maybe I can ask her who told her that dumb thing. I have to try to keep her talking, and I have to try to outthink her."

You could be forgiven if you thought that this monologue sounds contrived, but try to ignore the words and instead focus on the technique. The main goal here is to find a mechanism that helps the kid get past the physiological response so that she can focus on thinking. Kim might still end up turning around and beating as hasty a retreat as possible, but the difference is that it would be a conscious decision instead of a stimulus-response action.

The use of self-talk is more useful when the threat is not standing in front of you, threatening to rearrange your face. Self-talk is particularly useful when you are in an ongoing conflict, such as not getting along with a person you have to deal with regularly, or telling yourself that you *can* earn a passing mark on a difficult exam. In this sense, self-talk is simply the power of positive thinking made audible, and is a useful technique for dealing with the problem of a fight-freeze-flee response.

## Win-Lose, Lose-Lose, and Win-Win Scenarios

Competition in today's society is deeply ingrained, infusing virtually every human activity with an unrelenting hold. In a free-market economy, we lionize the companies that have risen to the top of the corporate heap, and success in business consists of beating the other guy to the consumer's wallet. Success in sports is predicated on winning it all, and all kinds of quotes are freely bandied about to justify winning. "Winning isn't everything, it's the only thing," "I'm with you win or tie," and "Nobody ever remembers who finished second." We compete to get into universities, to get a job, to advance in our careers, even to demonstrate how much better we are than others. We live in a world that seems intent on assigning us to one of two teams: the winners or the losers.

✦ **The win-lose scenario.** Little wonder then, that the most predominant conflict resolution strategy is the win-lose approach. This style is based on the expectation that there has to be a winner, and therefore a loser. Winning is seen as good and noble and admirable, while losing is viewed as abject failure, with the loser demonstrably less able than the winner.

It is also the win-lose approach that is most commonly seen among children in schools. Kids are taught to stick up for themselves, never to let anybody get the best of them, and if they have to fight, to make sure they get some good ones in. So teachers and principals everywhere, in trying to promote alternatives to win-lose, are squarely up against a society still very much tied to the notion of winning.

The fundamental flaw in the win-lose approach, besides its close proximity to anarchy, is the fact that it is almost never over after the initial conflict. Although the winner feels that he has proven his point to the loser and all other spectators, most losers can't seem to avoid the temptation of revenge. The kid who loses today will often bide his time to extract some measure of revenge later. This may be overt, in challenging the winner to another fight, or covert, in vandalizing his property or some other anonymous action. So, it's over then, right? Wrong.

When the former winner determines that it was an act of revenge, he similarly plots another act of revenge, and on and on it goes, with no clear end in sight. Note that this is unlike sports, where everyone plays by an agreed upon set of rules, where contravention of the rules is governed by a book and applied by an impartial judge, and where the nature and form of the conflict is confined. Interpersonal conflict is far more difficult to manage because, even if there were rules, no one could be compelled to follow them. What essentially occurs is that a win-lose scenario actually becomes a lose-lose scenario.

✦ **The lose-lose scenario.** Just as the term implies, nobody actually wins because of the damage that each inflicts on the other. We see this every day in schools. Alain calls Tony a jerk and Tony tells him what he can do to himself. Alain shoves Tony; Tony punches Alain. More screaming, more foul language. Alain tackles Tony; Tony kicks Alain in the face; Alain grabs a hockey stick; Tony attempts to choke Alain. The teacher arrives to find two snarling, bloodied, absolutely apoplectic boys threatening to kill each other. Lose-lose, and in a big way. Both are likely to be subject to whatever the most serious consequences are that can be applied; each is still angry with the other, and either or both may want to continue the battle in hopes of a decisive win.

Lose-lose scenarios also apply in the adult world. What else can a messy divorce be but lose-lose? While divorcing couples may intend to settle amicably, all of that goes out the window when the legal experts get involved. Then again, the legal system is by definition an adversarial system, another feature of our culture that stands as an impediment to peaceable conflict resolution.

✦ **The win-win scenario.** To even consider the possibility of a win-win situation demands the willing suspension of the need for total victory. Win-win scenarios further demand that both the participants give up some of what they want in order to gain most of what they want—each has to compromise. With more complex issues, a win-win solution involves collaboration and/or consensus. Either way, working toward a win-win solution is an important process for dealing with long-standing, deeply entrenched conflicts. There are other characteristics of a win-win approach, but for the most part, win-win approaches require:

   agreement to work together

   agreement as to the exact nature of the problem

   willingness to listen to each other's needs

   willingness to generate and discuss solutions

   willingness to give in order to get

If all of these preconditions are in place and there is honest and open communication, then a win-win solution is possible. This is particularly vital in relationships that are ongoing, such as those between spouses or partners, among kids and adults, among kids and kids, and among employers and employees. In relationships where there is no expectation of having to live or work with the other person, win-win scenarios are more difficult to enact; it might be convincingly argued that there is no incentive for a win-win solution if we never have to see that person again.

Regardless of the context of the conflict, be it a collective bargaining problem, a marital breakdown, or two kids fighting over who gets to use the computer, win-win should be the objective. If we somehow managed to persuade all children to use such an approach, the whole concept of winning at any cost would come under serious and critical scrutiny. We would find, perhaps, that when everybody wins, nobody loses. While this is an admittedly lofty goal, it is still worth striving for.

## Escalation of Conflict

When we are discussing conflict, I always ask my students to tell me what an escalator does. The answer is usually, "It takes you up," which is as simple and effective an answer as you can get. I then point out to them that petty conflicts can escalate very quickly until the result is usually some form of adult intervention. Out in the world, the same intervention is supplied by sometimes less-than-friendly members of the police force.

Like the fight-freeze-flee syndrome, the willingness to escalate petty conflicts is almost unconscious, and again appears to be rooted in the fear of being a loser. Nobody wants to come out on the losing end. Remember the silent movies of Laurel and Hardy? Those two comedians had a classic bit of visual comedy. It started with one doing something that injured or humiliated the other, then continued as the injured party did something back, only with a little more emphasis. Back and forth it went until it appeared that all-out war was about to begin. In the meantime, audiences laughed uproariously, and the escalation of conflict to some degree became legitimized through mass entertainment. Retaliation seemed to be both acceptable and funny.

To help kids deal with everyday conflict, it is helpful if they understand how and why conflict escalates, and how they can consciously de-escalate it so that problems are snuffed out before they reach thermonuclear proportions. While specific strategies will be spelled out in chapter 4, for now it is enough to know that a whole lot of the byproducts of conflict can be avoided by recognizing conflict and knowing how to short-circuit it.

## Conflict in the Classroom

There are a multiplicity of contributing factors to conflict in the classroom; most, but not all of which, involve interpersonal issues. The ways in which students are permitted to speak to and about one another can cause problems. If students are not corrected when they use demeaning language or give unfair criticism to their classmates, or if they are permitted to laugh at someone for making a mistake, the result is an emotionally unsafe environment. Kids who feel threatened when called upon to answer questions or offer opinions will simply remain silent, and by doing so fail to take advantage of opportunities to learn and grow. It is essential, then, for teachers to establish a classroom environment where each child is as free as possible from the threats of others.

Similarly, teachers need to examine their own methods of dealing with conflict. They must not advocate one way of doing things, then behave in a different way. If a teacher makes a serious issue out of no sarcasm in the classroom, all credibility spills out the door when he himself can't resist the urge to utter some snide remark to a student. If the same teacher insists that we talk our problems through, then he again loses credibility when he falls back on the authority of his position to decree a solution. This will be instantaneously observed by all but the most oblivious of students as being inconsistent and will be the source of some tension.

This is not to say that teachers can control the way in which interpersonal conflicts are played out. In fact, there is much that all but the most perceptive of teachers will never be aware of, simply because kids are adept at hiding whatever they don't want adults to see. Besides, the issue isn't about controlling conflict in the classroom, but with creating the kind of environment where the potential for positive interactions among kids is optimized and where there are mechanisms for the effective resolution of problems.

The fundamental objective in dealing with conflict in the classroom is to (1) create a supportive environment where every kid can feel safe, (2) empower kids to resolve their conflicts by introducing them to useful strategies for doing so, and (3) create the expectation of win-win solutions. In short, the classroom should be a safe, supportive place in which kids can work out their problems with each other. We have to ensure, however, that we have a clear vision of the goals of conflict resolution and the obstacles in the path before we begin employing whatever strategies are required.

# Misunderstandings About Conflict Resolution

Before talking about the goals of conflict resolution, it is first necessary to explore some common misunderstandings.

✦ **The objective of conflict resolution is victory.** In a narrow sense, this is true, but only if the result is mutually satisfactory. The ideal is a win-win solution.

✦ **Conflict can and should be eliminated, and if we just ignore it, it will go away.** Wrong on both counts. Conflict is as inevitable as sunrise; it can be managed but rarely controlled, and it can never be completely eliminated. Ignoring conflict simply avoids it, causes it to fester, and quite probably to increase over time.

✦ **Bullies have high self-esteem.** If high self-esteem accrues through intimidation, then yes, bullies *do* have self-esteem. But bullying actually has its roots in low self-esteem, in children who have been unable to achieve success through accepted, conventional means and who seek success in negative, antisocial ways.

✦ **Victims "bring it on themselves."** There are no human actions that can be used to justify abuse. Blaming the victim is all too common in our culture.

✦ **Adults should arbitrate in kids' conflicts.** Arbitration implies listening to the opposing views and then imposing a solution, which is almost never satisfactory to everyone subject to the edict. Mediation, on the other hand, helps kids to use resolution skills to solve their own problems.

There are probably other myths associated with people's ideas about conflict resolution, but the ones mentioned provide a useful framework for understanding how the goals of conflict resolution can sometimes become lost.

# Requirements for Conflict Resolution

To eliminate the type of thinking that is built on myths, the following goals form a basis for more effective conflict resolution:

+ **Conflict resolution requires a high degree of personal responsibility.** People need to take responsibility for their actions and to accept whatever consequences result. The goal, then, is to find a way of making kids aware of their personal responsibility, while at the same time encouraging them to accept such responsibility.

+ **Conflict resolution requires finding a zone of agreement.** Within almost every conflict there is some area of common agreement. The goal here is to find that zone and begin from there.

+ **Conflict resolution requires empathy and tolerance for others' views.** Empathy is the ability to understand others' views because of shared experience with the situation. Tolerance requires the willingness to accept the right of others to advocate conflicting views.

+ **Conflict resolution requires getting at the root cause of the conflict.** It is not unusual for conflict resolution to fail because a symptom of the problem has been attacked rather than its root cause. Taking a toy away from two squabbling children is a prime example. The problem is likely rooted in each child wanting to exert power and control over the other, but the adult seizes upon the toy as the problem and confiscates it. The conflict is resolved to the adult's satisfaction but certainly not to the toy's owner, who was unfairly treated, first by the other child and then by the adult.

+ **Conflict resolution requires the ability to separate the person from the problem.** There is no getting around the fact that most conflicts are highly emotional. Kids need to be shown how to focus on the nature of the conflict, not on the person. When we focus on "the person as the problem," we become too absorbed with the emotional interference set up by personality conflict to come to a rational solution.

If these requirements for conflict resolution are complex and difficult to master, they are made even more so when stacked against the many obstacles to effective conflict resolution. As if meeting the requirements wasn't difficult enough, there are at least ten actions people employ that sabotage conflict resolution or seriously impede it.

# Ten Ways to Fan the Flames of Conflict

1. **Yelling or shouting.** Kids who use this approach believe that he who hollers the loudest and shuts the other up is the winner. A raised voice is a de facto indicator of anger, and anger may lead to physical aggression. The person intimidated by yelling will often back off for fear of being the victim of physical retribution.

2. **Hitting, punching, slapping, and so on.** Some kids who are ill-equipped to engage in rational, verbal resolution of conflict will become incredibly frustrated. They will then lapse into the only way they can think of to protect themselves from being made to look foolish, which is to let their fists do the talking.

3. **Blaming someone or something else.** This is simply a refusal to take any kind of responsibility for an action. Conflict resolution is stalled because of those who refuse to accept that there really is a problem, or that they themselves are part of the problem.

4. **Name calling or using belittling language.** Kids who feel like they may be on the losing end will sometimes attempt to level the playing field by demeaning or belittling others. This creates another barrier to resolution.

5. **Refusing to listen, or ignoring.** Kids who act in this way have decided that they want no part of trying to solve what they see essentially as someone else's problem. As long as they don't have a problem, why should they even bother to listen to the other person?

6. **Threatening the other with dire consequences.** Kids utter threats because of their underlying belief that they can shut off the source of some anxiety (e.g., being shown that they are somehow wrong) through threats.

7. **Refusing to compromise.** Kids who refuse to compromise believe that if they yield even a fractional amount, they will suffer the eternal shame of losing. These kids are classic examples of those who view interpersonal relationships in win-lose terms.

8. **Using sarcasm or cynicism.** Sarcasm and cynicism perform two major functions: first, they trivialize what the other person views as important or useful; second, they devalue any attempt by the other person to act in good faith in seeking a resolution.

9. **Attempting to boss the other person.** Kids who do this view every situation as a power struggle and attempt to employ behaviors that they believe will control the other person.

10. **Walking or running away.** Kids who physically remove themselves from any attempt to achieve a negotiated settlement are employing the ultimate avoidance strategy.

There is a common thread to these ways of keeping conflict going. They all reflect a refusal by one party to accept even the remotest possibility of an amicable and fair solution. The combatant, for that is what he is, is satisfied to approach the situation as a win-lose proposition in which the one with the most power is the winner.

Another common thread deals with a refusal to accept responsibility. In a sense, this is also a refusal to acknowledge that there even *is* a problem. And if there is no problem, then why become involved in some sort of lame process for solving something that doesn't exit? These attitudes present mammoth obstacles in the way of helping kids deal with conflict.

## When Conflict Resolution Programs Fail

When your best efforts to improve students' conflict resolution skills fail, they do so in a decisive way, and it is helpful to examine why. First, it is crucial to think of conflict resolution not as a set of discrete actions or skills, but as something requiring healthy attitudes, basic skills, and a lot of practice.

✦ **Don't try to avoid touchy issues.** Instilling healthy attitudes in kids may be the most difficult of all tasks. Kids come to school with a variety of values and belief systems that are deeply etched into their psyches, and it is really difficult for teachers to modify kids' values and beliefs significantly. The most a teacher can hope for is to establish an environment of trust in which such issues as racism, sexism, homophobia, and interpersonal conflict are open for discussion. This will help correct one of the major problems that occurs when conflict resolution initiatives are taken—avoiding dealing with the difficult emotional issues that are the root cause of much conflict.

✦ **Don't impose solutions on kids.** A second way in which conflict resolution initiatives are sabotaged lies in the previously mentioned temptation of adults to impose solutions. When we put our practiced skills of problem analysis into motion, it is easy for us to see the usefulness of a particular solution; and because we want to spare the children the hassles of trying dead-end solutions, we impose the one we think will be best for them. All this does is reinforce the kids' belief that they are incapable and that it is the adult (power figure) who determines the solution. They also miss the opportunity to practice problem-solving skills.

✦ **Don't make all of kids' decisions for them.** A third reason why conflict resolution programs sometimes fail is kids' poorly developed decision-making skills. Both teachers and parents have a deep and generally protective interest in the growth and development of children. They will often do whatever they can to shield kids from things they think will be too difficult for them and will preempt kids' decision making in order to protect them. This is a natural response, but not especially helpful to kids. Much of the conflict in our lives is, and will continue to be, interpersonal. This means that every child requires the ability to make decisions and solve problems effectively. Adults—teachers and parents included—need to let kids make their own decisions and even to let them fail.

✦ **Don't underemphasize the need for self-esteem.** A fourth way in which conflict resolution programs can falter relates to the varying levels of each child's self-esteem. To teach someone how to be assertive assumes that that person possesses enough confidence and a sufficiently healthy self-image to actually put assertiveness into practice. Invariably, kids with high levels of self-esteem will be quick to learn and implement conflict resolution strategies, while those with low levels will not. This is somewhat ironic, as it is the kids with low levels of self-esteem who need those strategies the most. Therefore, any program aimed at finding better ways to resolve conflict must create a safe and supportive classroom environment through:

✧ instilling healthy attitudes about conflict and being willing to talk about difficult emotional issues

✧ providing opportunities for kids to make decisions

✧ enhancing every participant's self-esteem

Nobody said that teaching kids better ways of resolving conflict was going to be easy, but it certainly remains one of the most important things we can do.

## Ideas for Helping Kids Resolve Conflict

Assuming that we have been successful in instilling essential attitudes in kids, the following strategies may be helpful. They may be used alone or in combination, but they are predicated on the assumption that both kids in a conflict are willing to work together to solve the problem.

✦ **Agree to take turns.** As simple as it sounds, taking turns requires each kid to give up a little. It still must be determined who gets the first turn, but if there is already agreement to take turns, the rest should be relatively easy.

✦ **Agree to let chance decide.** This could be flipping a coin or drawing straws. Once again, success depends on a willingness to abide by the outcome.

✦ **Agree to get help.** This is an admission of an impasse, but also indicates a willingness to seek another solution. The helper can be an adult, who must be careful not to impose a solution, or a peer helper/mediator. The use of trained peer helpers—kids helping kids arrive at solutions of their own— can be really effective.

✦ **Agree to compromise.** This assumes that both kids are willing to give up something, usually something more complex than simple, tangible things like basketballs, using the computer, or a seat on the school bus.

✦ **Apologize.** This is a very powerful way to defuse a conflict, but should only be used when one child actually did something wrong and/or hurtful. Apologies indicate one person's willingness to take responsibility and offer an olive branch. An apology frequently ends a conflict then and there.

✦ **Avoid.** This is not a particularly good option when the conflict is with someone you must deal with on a continual basis, because it allows the conflict to fester. Avoidance can be useful when the conflict is with someone you will never have to deal with again, like a rude clerk at the store, a greedy slob in the buffet line, or a crotchety neighbor.

✦ **Use self-deprecating humor.** Humor and laughter are often effective in relieving the tension arising from conflict. But a kid using this strategy should be sure not to aim the humor at anyone but himself.

✦ **Give in.** Kids should do this only after they have undertaken a quick "cost-benefit analysis." They should decide if the issue is worth going to the wall over, and if it isn't, they should give their antagonists what they want. This is not being passive; it is being pragmatic.

The most crucial aspect to any of these strategies is that kids be receptive to the idea that conflicts can be resolved without using force, without resorting to win-lose tactics, and without escalating the conflict through verbal or physical aggression. If kids buy into this approach, they are on their way to dealing with the ever-present conflicts in their day-to-day lives.

## A Vision of the Possible

It isn't easy being a kid today. The world we live in is undergoing rapid and overwhelming social and technological change. Insidious influences, from popular entertainment and network news to sensationalist newspapers and the behavior of our leaders, assail our minds from every direction. It is difficult enough to carve out some sort of meaning for ourselves as adults; imagine what it must be like for kids.

As teachers and parents, we have to find ways of meeting our kids' needs for safety, for acceptance, for belonging, and for resolving conflicts in ways that are positive and productive. We have to make them aware of conflict—where it comes from, how it escalates, and what they can do to de-escalate it. We have to sell them on the idea that win-win solutions are always best because they mean that both sides of any conflict get most of what they want. Giving a little to get most of what is wanted is preferable to the risk of losing everything.

We want to instill in kids behaviors and attitudes that reflect the belief that all others are capable and worthwhile. We want to help kids become optimistic instead of pessimistic, to be open to new ideas rather than tied to existing ones, to view the glass as half full instead of half empty. We want kids who are able to negotiate from a position of confidence rather than be entrenched in their positions because of fear.

Finally, we want kids to be able to approach any kind of conflict with the confidence and self-assurance that they can and will arrive at a solution. Put simply, we want to snatch them out of the jaws of the dragon and teach them to ride it.

# 2.

# Self-esteem:
# To Bottle the Wind

## About Kenny

A couple of years ago, a twelve-year-old named Kenny enrolled in our school at the beginning of September. He'd lived his whole life with his mother and stepfather in another city, but had decided to come and live with a father he'd only seen a dozen or so times in his life. When she brought Kenny in to register him, his stepmother told us that he'd be trouble, so we weren't surprised when he showed almost immediate signs of aggression, unwillingness to comply with his teacher's expectations, and inappropriate attention-seeking behavior.

As the weeks and months wore on, he was spending more and more time sitting on a bench outside the office looking forlorn. I spent hours with him, trying to get at the heart of what was making him behave the way he did. It seemed to me that he felt controlled by his behavior and had no idea how to help himself. I didn't view his behavior as a personal affront, though it was apparent his teacher did.

During one particularly candid session, Kenny cried when he began to tell me about the treatment he'd received from his mother and stepfather. To say that their discipline was overly harsh was to say that there is sand in the Sahara. Groundings were as long as one or two months, and during those times he was confined to his room, unable to listen to radio, watch TV, or communicate with anyone in the family. He was allowed to come out for dinner, but had to wash all the dishes before returning to his room. If he broke a dish, he was screamed at for being stupid and clumsy. He thought of himself as a really bad kid.

Kenny told me he had had no friends at school, which was confirmed by a phone call to his former counselor. The other boys had ostracized and bullied him and one evening showed up outside his house where they proceeded to throw rocks at his bedroom window, finally shattering it. Kenny's mother and stepfather, rather than providing the loving support and help that most caring adults would, told him that if he were a better person, other kids would like him. Then they made him pay for the window.

Kenny admitted that he was afraid he'd have to go back to his mother's house; his mother had told him that if he was bad at school that year, he'd have to return because this would show that his father obviously couldn't handle him. That was when he told me that his stepfather sometimes hit him. I phoned the Ministry of Social Services, and they put a social worker on the case. Kenny's father came in later and told me that he had no idea what Kenny had been subjected to, and that he'd make darn sure Kenny never had to go back. Meanwhile, the social worker did whatever social workers do and Kenny began to feel a sense of relief.

I would love to be able to report that Kenny's life turned around that year, but it didn't. The rest of the year saw only minor improvements, and Kenny still spent most afternoons on the bench outside my office. Knowing his life history, and feeling somewhat protective of him, I spent more time than I could really afford talking with him, building him up, giving him ideas about how to deal with others. He eventually came to trust me and would often come to talk to me. I tried to help him develop what he so obviously lacked—self-esteem.

Kenny's low self-esteem had developed through repeated experiences that sent a variety of implied messages. He was told and shown that he was not capable of normal or good behavior; so he had no confidence that he could be successful. He didn't feel loved and accepted within his own family, much less among his peers. He didn't feel physically, emotionally, or psychologically safe, since he knew that he couldn't rely on *anybody to come to his rescue. Nothing in his life had shown him that he was valued or important. Faced with such constant negative and ambivalent messages, Kenny arrived at a view of himself as a bad person—incapable of learning, incapable of getting along, and essentially unlikable.*

*Thankfully, there is a happy ending. Kenny's father had been an accomplished high school wrestler and had kept in touch with the wrestling coach at the nearby high school. He went to the coach and asked him if he would work with Kenny when the boy started high school the following September. Kenny discovered something he could do, and that he could do exceptionally well. Within months of taking up the sport, Kenny won medals at the Northern B.C. Winter Games. Further, his marks improved, he made friends, and he became much happier. He discovered that he was capable, that he was accepted, that he was safe, and that he was valued for what he could do. Success is a powerful antidote to the poison of low self-esteem.*

## What Is Self-esteem?

In the past several years, much has been said and written about self-esteem and its importance to positive mental health. And for good reason. We now understand that how we feel about ourselves has a major impact on our performance—whether on the job, at home, in the classroom, or in social situations. Self-esteem can be characterized as the degree to which we feel:

+ **capable and confident.** These feelings come as a result of achieving success and for being recognized for it. With children, it is not just the *product* that determines success, but may also be the child's effort, willingness to try, and persistence.

+ **loved, accepted, and that we belong.** These feelings come with unconditional love, acceptance, and respect. We can make kids feel these emotions through our constant support and by giving them opportunities to make choices and decisions without excessive criticism when mistakes are inevitably made.

- **safe.** Safety has physical, emotional, and psychological aspects. Frightened people seldom perform well. Children must be made to feel safe about making mistakes, safe from threats of ridicule, and safe from loss of emotional security.

- **valued and important.** We can instill these feelings in children by listening to them, considering their views, recognizing their help within the family and in the classroom, and by asking them for their thoughts and paying attention to what they think.

There are two important concepts to consider when trying to build kids' self-esteem. First, feelings of self-esteem must be internalized. Telling a kid how good he is is useless unless he actually believes it. Second, each child's level of self-esteem will vary, depending on a variety of factors. These include how familiar he is with a task or situation and how comfortable he is with his peers, teacher, and parents. It will also vary with his comfort level with the unknown or with uncertainty. Even kids with generally high levels of self-esteem may experience misgivings or a crisis in confidence in a new or strange environment.

One prevalent myth concerning self-esteem is that highly successful people are automatically endowed with high self-esteem. In many cases this may be true, but in many more it is not. Athletes and entertainers who possess natural gifts to excite and entertain people have the luxury of constant, overwhelming external affirmation. They come to depend on the adulation and the applause and to rely on it as a measure of their competence. Many of these people never internalize a sense of personal capability and so cannot feed their own egos. This is why retired athletes and "cold" entertainers frequently descend into their own private versions of hell. Drugs, alcohol, marital problems, lost fortunes, and an inability to reenter mainstream life are all at least partly attributable to an inability to self-generate feelings of personal worth.

Self-esteem cannot be bottled and sold, and we cannot give it to someone as we would present them with a birthday gift. Though the development of self-esteem takes place over a lifetime of experience, it is enhanced by success and the affirmation of success, both from external influences and from within the individual. We must recognize what self-esteem sounds and looks like before we embark on any mission to enhance it.

## What Does Self-esteem Sound Like?

Apart from the clues we pick up from a child's behavior, many clues to how children view themselves can be heard in what they say. Here are some typical statements that reflect both high and low levels of self-esteem:

| *High Self-esteem* | *Low Self-esteem* |
|---|---|
| Kids who say: | Kids who say: |
| "I think I can do that." | "I can't do that." |
| "I will ..." | "I won't ..." |
| "I'm as smart as anybody." | "I'm not very smart." |
| "If I ask, they might let me." | "There's no use even asking." |
| "I have lots of friends." | "Nobody likes me." |
| "I'll do better next time." | "I won't do that again." |
| "Can I help you?" | "Do I have to help you?" |
| "I don't understand this." | "This is stupid." |
| "I look okay today." | "I'm ugly." |

So why such a dramatic difference? It might be that the child with high self-esteem has been brought up in an environment where he came to internalize feelings of self-worth by being made to feel capable, accepted, safe, and valued. And this probably helped him achieve success, which further contributed to the upward spiral of self-esteem.

The child with low self-esteem, on the other hand, feels neither capable nor accepted, neither safe nor valued. He fears failing because of failure's unpleasant consequences—criticism from the people who count most in his life or ridicule from his peers. In any event, it becomes easier for him to adopt a negative, sometimes cynical and sarcastic veneer, to mask his true feelings of inadequacy. Sadly, this is not exclusive to childhood; countless adults with low self-esteem behave in exactly the same way.

## What Does Low Self-esteem Look Like?

There are any number of behaviors that are frequently seen in children with low self-esteem. Here are some of them:

+ **Reluctance to try new or different things.** These children lack confidence and feel uncertain or incapable. They are afraid of making a mistake, perhaps due to the negative feedback they received, especially from their parents and teachers, whenever they made errors.

+ **Quick frustration from a lack of immediate success or understanding.** Such frustration is typically expressed in one of two ways: tears or displays of anger, including yelling, slamming things, and violence directed at others (usually weaker persons—brothers and sisters are favorite targets). Lack of success affirms their already low opinion of their capabilities.

+ **Bullying behavior.** Children who are unable to achieve success in positive and socially acceptable ways will sometimes resort to bullying others. Bullies attempt to raise their own levels of self-esteem by making others feel bad. In effect, they steal self-esteem from others and receive affirmation for their success by making others react negatively to them.

+ **Attitudes that are hypercritical and negative, sarcastic and cynical.** These attitudes are sometimes adopted as an attempt to compensate for lack of confidence. Kids with these attitudes tend to disparage the success or quality of other people and things.

+ **Withdrawal, depression, and inability or unwillingness to communicate.** These children have no idea how to cope or even that they can cope; they feel both powerless and hopeless in taking control of the things that affect their lives. These symptoms spell *danger*, and contain real potential for self-harm.

+ **Blaming behavior.** For these kids, assigning fault is a big issue; fault equals failure, and failure has been internalized as bad, stupid, unacceptable, or all three. The sentiment might be, "since I have no control over my actions, it can't be my fault."

+ **Dependency on others to tell them what to do, what is good, and what is acceptable.** Having come to depend on external validation, these kids have only a fuzzy idea of what normal is; so they defer to the dominant people in their lives.

+ **Lying and/or stealing.** Lying is usually an indicator of a child's desire to avoid unpleasant consequences, but it is also part of a desire not to have to accept fault. Stealing may be associated with the need for power, especially for kids who feel essentially powerless in most areas of their lives.

+ **Disobedience and noncompliance with authority despite repeated punishment or application of consequences.** These kids don't know how to control their behavior and rarely recognize the connection between an act and its consequences. They believe they have no control, and since they view themselves as bad kids, their misbehavior is inevitable. Sometimes, too, their behavior may be so controlled at home that in the less punitive environment of school, misbehavior isn't as big a risk.

+ **Adoption of dangerous and/or self-destructive behavior.** All parents worry about their children running with the wrong crowd, experimenting with drugs and alcohol, and engaging in sexual activity at too early an age. Kids who end up doing these things are looking to their peer group to fulfill their needs for safety, belonging, acceptance, and worthiness.

All in all, these visual indicators of low self-esteem, coupled with the words and sentiments they express, indicate children who are experiencing alarming levels of powerlessness, helplessness, and hopelessness. If we, as their teachers and parents, can counteract these feelings, we will be able to help these children develop feelings of healthy self-esteem, with all of the positive benefits that will accrue.

## The Benefits of High Self-esteem

Though the benefits of high self-esteem are legion, most or all fall within the following six categories.

1. **Ability to resist negative peer pressure.** There is a clear relationship between self-esteem and susceptibility to peer pressure. Simply put, the higher the level of self-esteem, the lower the susceptibility to peer pressure, and vice versa.

2. **Development of personal power.** High self-esteem equals greater personal power and strength of character, which equip kids to resist bullying and put-downs from others. If we accept that virtually all conflict stems from an imbalance of power, then it is vital to help kids develop as much personal power as possible.

3. **Selection of worthy friends.** In many ways the old truism that "like attracts like" is essentially true for most people. Kids with high self-esteem typically seek out others with similar feelings of competence. And kids with low self-esteem generally find each other and feed off the negative vibrations of their group. Self-esteem also influences kids' relationships with their peers and adults and, when they grow up, their selection of a spouse.

4. **Development of positive attitudes toward work and achievement.** If children feel competent and confident, they won't easily give up. They'll have a healthy attitude toward work and an expectation of success.

5. **Development of potential for creativity, emotional equilibrium, and happiness.** Success leads to feelings of capability and competence, which encourage people to push themselves, to take risks, to try the unfamiliar, and as a result, to increase their opportunities for learning and for success.

6. **Development of positive character traits.** These include honesty, loyalty, integrity, compassion, tolerance, and "doing the right thing." People with high self-esteem know they have nothing to lose and nothing to fear from displaying these characteristics. Fear often motivates people with low self-esteem to withdraw into self-created safety zones.

In helping a child develop self-esteem, parents and educators must first have a positive vision of the child, a vision that sees him as a happy and well-adjusted person. This requires creating an environment where self-esteem is enhanced and maintained. But, if self-esteem can't be bottled and sold, how do we go about creating such an environment? Perhaps the following ideas may be useful.

## Creating the Environment

To develop any kind of competence, it is first necessary to ensure that the right environment exists. Self-esteem is impossible to build if the physical, emotional, and psychological environments are contradictory to the essential conditions required. Three elements—mind-set, modeling, and methods—are essential if self-esteem is to be positively influenced.

### Mind-set

Many, many years ago, at parent-teacher interview time, a father described his approach to raising kids: "It's just like training a dog," he said. "You feed 'em, show 'em what to do, and you smack 'em until they get it right." I thought he was kidding. Then the hairs on the back of my neck stood up when I realized he wasn't. His attitude went a long way to explaining why his son was so easily frustrated, afraid of making mistakes, and reluctant to try anything new or difficult.

The fact is that raising children should not be anything like training an animal; children have the capacity to reason, to make decisions, to think in abstract terms, and to learn from their mistakes without being smacked to reinforce the learning. That father, whose views were probably quite extreme, was nevertheless a prime example of "wrong mind-set."

Mind-set (or attitude) comprises the sum total of the ways in which we think—about ourselves, about others, about authority, and about children. And our actions stem from our beliefs and values, which are based on past experience. This is why we, as parents, tend either to mimic the ways in which we were raised or pointedly avoid them. So, our first task is to eliminate outmoded or negative ways of thinking about children and the ways in which they should be raised. Some of these outmoded ideas include the following:

✦ **Children should be seen and not heard.** Bunk! Eventually, children who don't have the chance to be heard won't be seen much either. This sentiment attempts to control children's behavior by pulling rank. It often results in intense rebellion in adolescence.

✦ **Children must be shielded from negative influences.** In some situations, yes, but the ideal is to teach children how to recognize and to resist negative influences. Parents who try to control who their children associate with in the neighborhood and at school may think that they are helping their children, but they are not.

✦ **Children must always obey and respect their elders.** This is fine as far as it goes, but children may encounter "elders" in their lives who treat them badly. To insist on obedience and respect for those who treat us poorly reinforces the notion that adult authority is unquestionable and that power belongs to the biggest and strongest.

✦ **Children who are punished for disobedience are not likely to repeat it.** If this were so, no child would disobey more than once. The whole issue of consequences for misbehavior or noncompliance is a slippery one. The ideal is to make behavioral expectations and negative consequences clearly known and then stress that behavior is a conscious decision. Therefore, if the child chooses to do something wrong knowing the consequence, then he is, in fact, accepting the consequence.

When the parent or teacher determines and applies a consequence, with no involvement by or explanation to the child, the child often feels little or no connection between the act and the consequence. Instead of the child learning self-discipline, the message is that discipline is something applied by someone else.

✦ **Children are empty vessels who need to be taught the right way to behave.** Again, fine as far as it goes. Where this breaks down is when subsequent experience reveals that such teachings are unacceptable to others. For example, if a child's parents teach him to beat up anyone who threatens him, or to ostracize those who don't conform to his parents' views of acceptability, or to demean or devalue those who don't agree with him, the child will become bewildered when he finds himself in trouble with his peers, his teacher, the neighbors, or with others.

As parents and teachers it is critical that our mind-set be directed toward raising children who are capable of self-discipline, of awareness and tolerance of the differences among people, of the ability to recognize and resist negative influences, and of personal responsibility. If our mind-sets are further directed at an optimistic view of children as being capable, then we should be able to guide them from the side, rather than lead them from the front.

## Modeling

As much as we may like to, we can't control everything our children learn. They learn about the world and how it works by watching, listening, and emulating the most dominant adults in their lives—with teachers and parents usually at the top of the list. In "behavior-speak," this is known as modeling. As parents and teachers, we often see our own behavior—tone of voice, body language, and other habits—in our children. Sometimes we like what we see and reinforce the kids for it; other times we cringe when we realize they've picked up some aspect we'd rather they hadn't.

There is really nothing we can do to prevent children from consciously and unconsciously absorbing many of our characteristics; it is how we learned from our parents and how they learned from theirs and so on. Thus, it is important that we try, as much as possible, to be positive models, because, like it or not, we are their first and most important role models. Here are some of the things we model for kids:

✦ **How to express anger and frustration.** Negative expressions of these emotions include verbally lashing out, yelling, throwing things, slamming doors, becoming verbally aggressive, walking out, pouting, or refusing to speak. If you are the type to scream, stomp out of the room, and slam the door on your way out, don't be at all surprised if your beloved child adopts the same strategy when the conflicts of adolescence rear their ugly heads. Let's hope that, as adults, we can manage our anger in such a way that we are observed as calm, rational, and accepting.

+ **How to deal with failure or mistakes.** Negative models include refusal to acknowledge error (sometimes with great vehemence and lack of reason), blaming someone or something else, or by venting our anger. Kids need to see adults acknowledging and admitting their mistakes and need to hear adults apologizing when they have hurt someone. If you avoid personal responsibility for mistakes and errors, your children will too.

+ **How to view others.** Essentially, there are two ways of viewing others: first, with acceptance, seeing the existence of (or potential for) goodness and capability in them; and second, from a deficiency point of view, which sees others as "less than" and worthy only of criticism or, worse, ridicule. Those who behave in the second way often become hypercritical malcontents, while those who accept people for who they are become optimistic and generally content.

+ **How to view authority.** This is a tough one, because there are times in life when authority figures don't treat people very kindly. We can choose to be unquestionably compliant, openly rebellious, covertly rebellious, or ambivalent. Whichever you choose, be aware that your attitudes will become mirrored by your kids. Thus, if you are always talking about what a jerk your boss is, then your child is apt to express the same kind of sentiments about his teacher or principal. Overall, kids need to be made aware that, unless we are born king or queen, there will always be someone with greater authority than us; so we'd better learn to cope.

+ **How to express humor.** More fights start among kids over differences in what each considers funny than almost anything else. The type of humor that is especially dangerous is that based on ridicule, having fun at the expense of others and seeing others as deficient. The most common response given by perpetrators of scraps is, "but I was just teasing [having fun]." These kids are genuinely confused when the object of the fun became angry enough to go for the throat. Similarly, humor rooted in sexism, racism, or homophobia increases the potential for sudden and violent response.

+ **Predisposition toward activity or passivity.** If adults are the type to sit idly by and complain about everything with sarcasm and cynicism, so will their kids. Adults who are moved to act, and who set out to change the things that bother them, demonstrate to their children that we can either sit and whine or take control.

There are many other behaviors that kids model. How you relate to people and what you say about them is important. So is your own attitude toward work. In all things, teachers and parents in particular must work hard to ensure a match between what we say and what we do, and to try to avoid saying and doing the things we don't want our children to say and do.

If we are sincere about wanting to create an environment in which our kids can develop healthy levels of self-esteem, we have to look at the components of that kind of environment. Too often, when our kids are struggling, we look everywhere but at ourselves. By giving serious thought to our own mind-sets, and by becoming aware of the incredible power of our own modeling, we can begin to develop methods for helping our children develop self-esteem.

## Methods—How Teachers Can Help Kids Develop Self-esteem

Society entrusts teachers with massive responsibilities. Teachers are expected to fill children with facts and figures, with knowledge of processes and technology, with manual skills, and with the ability to function well in a free and democratic society. Whew! Is that all? Little wonder that teachers and administrators everywhere are scrambling to try to meet the demands. Sadly, the pressure to do it all often results in classrooms that are completely task-oriented, with little time left for students' personal and social development.

Despite the existence of the "all business" classroom, many others are entirely different. Teachers in those classrooms understand that a precondition of learning is the creation of an environment that is supportive, humane, and cognizant of the differing needs of the students. They also understand that enhancing students' self-esteem cannot be accomplished through a series of logically connected lessons, as this is a developmental process that evolves through daily modeling and is maintained by faithful adherence to common ideals. Such ideals must be articulated, modeled, and repeated with enough frequency that they become the standard way-of-work for the class.

### Classroom "Best Practices"

A good place to begin is by forming a list of classroom "best practices"—just another term for rules. For example:

✦ **We do not laugh at others' errors.** Kids need to learn the difference between sharing a laugh over something funny and laughing at someone who has made a mistake.

✦ **Everyone has the right to be left alone if he wants.** Students have to understand that when someone says to leave him alone, he means just that. And the request must be respected.

✦ **All points of view have a right to be heard.** Everyone has the right to express an opinion and should not be attacked if it happens to be unpopular. Teachers can model this by calmly accepting all opinions from students.

As an example: A student says he thinks that math is stupid and doesn't see why he has to learn it. The reactive teacher responds with anger, indignation, or sarcasm, thereby demonstrating to the student that his view is worthless. The supportive teacher might thank the student for his view, explain that he can probably understand why the kid thinks that, and then state his own position without demeaning the student. This teacher is calm, empathetic, but assertive in stating his disagreement.

✦ **Teasing is permissible only if the recipient says it is.** Teasing becomes more tedious with time, and students often become extremely upset if the joke goes on too long. Some kids don't seem to mind, but most dislike being teased if they believe it is intended to demean them.

✦ **Name-calling is not permitted.** When students disagree with each other, name-calling frequently occurs, generally started by the one who can't think of anything else to say. Name-calling is an aggressive act, which can rapidly escalate conflict. It is therefore taboo.

✦ **Resolving differences never includes physical contact, except perhaps shaking hands.** Acts of physical violence are never acceptable.

✦ **Each student has equal rights and responsibilities.** Kids are very concerned with rights, but less so with responsibilities. The teacher has to work hard to convince kids that the two are inextricably related.

✦ **No student may take or borrow the belongings of others without permission.** Nor may they hide, damage, or destroy the belongings of others.

It is not enough to merely post such behavioral ideals on the wall for future reference. Just as students will model the values, beliefs, and behaviors they are exposed to at home, so too will they absorb the traits of their teachers, especially in elementary grades where much of each day is spent with the same adult. Teachers must be acutely aware of the impact their words and actions have on student behavior. Setting the tone is only half the battle; modeling the behaviors is even more important.

To build a supportive environment, teachers have to avoid the use of sarcasm, an artless form of humor that kids master in about fifteen minutes. Teachers must also avoid cynicism, as well as unwelcome nicknames or put-downs, either subtle or blatant. The teacher who displays these qualities hasn't a leg to stand on when kids treat each other in the same way. Teachers must demonstrate through word and deed a commitment to an open, non-conflictual classroom, one in which kids will feel safe from any form of abuse.

## Additional Strategies for Teachers

✦ **Use praise and encouragement lavishly, but specifically.** Blanket praise misses the mark. If we commend the whole class, the lower achieving student doesn't believe it because he knows he isn't doing well, and the quicker student doesn't buy it because he knows that there are a number of kids who are doing nothing. Similarly, blanket blame doesn't work either, because it's likely that only a few are guilty, but the rest will have to suffer.

+ **Look for the good in your students.** A test score of 90 out of 100 means ninety *correct*, not ten wrong. Try not to focus on deficiencies; few, if any, people have ever dramatically improved by being told how inept they were. The emphasis must be on building students up by emphasizing their successes, which we hope they'll internalize as healthier self-esteem.

+ **Make a big deal out of students' out-of-school successes.** Just as teachers are people with outside lives and interests, so too are kids. Make a point of finding out about the things they are involved in, and use their successes to boost their confidence and sense of accomplishment.

+ **Offer students' options in their everyday work.** This might include a choice of topics for a report, methods of presenting it to the class, or opting to take on work for extra credit. Giving students choices gives them practice in using the mental processes required in making decisions.

+ **Emphasize that it is only necessary for students to do *their* best, not to be *the* best.** Students who are highly competitive and always have to be the best are often headed for a fall. Sooner or later they will run into someone who does something just a little bit better and just a little bit quicker. I have seen these kids genuinely depressed when they scored *only* 96 percent on a math test. It's great to strive to become better, but not if the intent is to "beat" everyone else.

+ **Be quick to forgive and don't hold grudges.** The kid who seriously messes up in the morning should be dealt with appropriately, and that should be the end of it. A teacher I once knew would sneer at a certain student with a look of unconcealed disgust for days after he had done something to breach the rules of the classroom. This approach helps no one.

+ **Use discipline that is fair.** Fair does not mean equal; fair means appropriate to the child and to the act. The circumstances, past history, sequence of events leading up to the misbehavior, and degree of willfulness must all be weighed to arrive at discipline that is fair for that particular child.

### Some Instructional Strategies

Direct instructional strategies work only in the presence of the strong, supportive environment already detailed. Many of the following ideas are direct, but some are subtle; part of an overall strategy of creating an esteem-building environment. Here are some examples:

+ **Icebreaker activity.** This helps build a supportive environment and gives students the opportunity to find others with shared experiences. It also helps students develop a sense of belonging to the group.

Create a list of twenty experiences that one or more of your students are likely to have had and print a copy for each student. The task is for each student to go around the room talking to others in order to find at least one person whose experience fits each statement and then to write the names of the students beside the appropriate statements. If you happen to know of an experience that one of your shy, reluctant students has had, be sure to include that on the list. Sample statements look like this:

Find someone who has:

caught a fish larger than 2 kilograms (4.4 pounds)

ever had his picture in the newspaper

won first place in a competition

been in an airplane

his own bank account

After the task is completed, go over each statement orally with the group, identifying those students to whom that statement relates. Use this opportunity to praise, encourage, and build self-image. You will be surprised at some of the accomplishments of your students, and so will their classmates.

+ **"I like, I don't like" activity.** To help kids focus on what they *can* do instead of what they *can't* do, have them each take a piece of paper and divide it into two vertical columns. The heading for the left column is "Things I Like About Me," and for the right, "Things I Don't Like About Me."

Try to have them focus on their talents, abilities, personal qualities, and positive habits, not on their possessions as in "I like my shoes" or "I like my Nintendo." This should elicit responses such as "I'm good in math," "I'm really gentle with little children," or "I do my homework without being told."

On the "I Don't Like" list, ask the kids to cross out or erase anything over which they have no control, such as "I don't like it that my parents split up," "I don't like the way my ears stick out," or "I don't like being the oldest kid in my family." To focus on these is to focus on the generally impossible, so there is no sense spending time thinking about them.

Direct your students' attention to the things they can reasonably change, and make it clear that change in some things is inevitably slow. Make sure they understand that they are the ones who have control and that you are there to help them, as much as you can, to change the things they don't like. Obviously, this is not a one-shot lesson, taught and forgotten. Rather, it helps to lay a positive foundation for students' future successes.

+ **"I can do, I wish I could do" activity.** This can be used as either an alternative or as an extension of the above activity. It is almost exactly the same as the previous activity, but uses the headings "I Can Do" and "I Wish I Could Do." This activity may be less judgmental than the previous activity, since "like" and "dislike" are value-laden sentiments. Before using either activity, think about the readiness of your students to understand and accept the task.

+ **Student oral reporting.** In this activity the task is for each student to design and deliver a five- to eight-minute oral report. The structure is that of a how-to report, and students are invited to use any props they like. Be prepared; students may bring their pet rabbit, a doghouse they built, enough panzerotti for the class, or just about anything.

The benefits for students are many: they get to showcase something they know or do very well; they are affirmed for their success, both by the teacher and their peers; public feedback is given for their efforts; and a supportive environment is created. These don't necessarily build self-esteem, but the odds are good that they will.

From a teacher's perspective, the task has to be structured carefully. Here are some ideas:

*Task:* To deliver a five- to eight-minute oral report.

*Topic:* How to do something that you already know how to do well.

*Props:* Models, samples, examples, charts, photos, equipment, finished products, and so on. *Other:* You may use the chalkboard, overhead projector, lectern, audiovisual equipment, or any other equipment available.

*Also:* Be prepared to field questions from the audience, and prepare three to five questions to quiz your listeners.

Teachers can increase chances for success by selecting the first four or five reporters from their most confident and able students. These will set the tone for subsequent reports by showing panic-stricken students how it can be done. A final, vital aspect to this activity is that you give a quick critique that focuses *only on the positive aspects* following each report. The point, after all, is to help your students feel a sense of success, which we hope they will internalize. Finally, tell students that you will give them their marks (perhaps out of 25 or 30) privately; it's up to them to decide if they want to share their marks with their peers.

✦ **Buddying with another class.** Helping younger students through regular, weekly buddy reading can not only help the little kids, but can also be a confidence builder for the older students. There are a number of spinoffs, including the development of your students' supportive, nurturing skills and the feelings of self-worth that accrue from helping someone younger learn or helping them out on the schoolyard when they have conflicts. It can be startling to see some of your struggling students become excellent big buddies, but it shouldn't be. Often these kids have firsthand knowledge of what it is to struggle, so they have an innate sense of what the younger ones need. Just make sure you constantly affirm their successes. A final note: buddying can be used for many activities other than reading; it can be used for writing (letters to Santa is a great experience), for P.E. activities, for concert productions, and for general tutoring of the little ones.

+ **Create a "service to the school" ethic.** Make it abundantly clear that good citizenship includes service to others with no expectation of reward. Encourage kids to help in the school. Teacher-librarians can always use student help for carding and shelving books. Individual teachers have numerous classroom housekeeping duties. Some schools have peer-helping or peer-mediation programs, which train senior students to help others solve their problems. Students who commit to service to the school must be encouraged and given a lot of recognition; volunteering is one more way kids can develop their self-esteem.

+ **Use wall space to display all students' work.** Sometimes teachers make the mistake of exhibiting only the best work on the walls. However, there are some kids who will never paint a wonderful picture or write an outstanding story. In my experience, overpraising the work of the gifted has never motivated the rest to strive for perfection. Display every-one's work; often the mere knowledge that the work will be displayed motivates kids to do better than they'd normally do. They should be competing with themselves to improve, not trying to meet some benchmark they see as unreasonably high.

+ **Create an "All About Us" photo board.** If space and finances permit, reserve one classroom bulletin board for photos of your students. We are not talking here about the formal portraits done each school year by commercial photographers. We are talking about candid shots of the students actually doing things in and around the school. By seeing themselves accomplishing things, students have visual evidence that they are indeed capable.

+ **Create class legends and traditions.** Just as families have legends and traditions, so too should a class group of students. Funny incidents, great accomplishments, and notable skill in any curricular area can all form the basis for legends and traditions. Some teachers devote the last five minutes of the day to a class discussion on the good things that happened that day, a strategy intended to send the kids home in a positive frame of mind. Instead of focusing on the fact that the science experiment was a colossal failure, kids can choose to recall that they helped the kindergarten class make valentines.

✦ **Recognize when you need to move the goal posts closer.** By this I mean that there will be students in your class who will struggle for weeks, meeting failure every day, and losing. Instead of lamenting what they can't do, focus your energies on giving them the kind of tasks that will show what they *can* do. So much of achieving success depends on our mind-set at the beginning of a task; if we undertake an assignment with feelings of doubt and uncertainty that we won't be able to do it, chances are excellent we will fulfill our own prophecy. With low achievers, their sense of self-assurance must be built before their academic performance can be improved, and self-assurance can't be built if they are continually given tasks they know they can't do.

## *In a Nutshell: Developing Self-esteem in the Classroom*

By now it is more than apparent that nurturing self-esteem in the classroom is of paramount importance. To do so teachers have to act positively to create and build a supportive, caring environment in which opportunities for student success and recognition are abundant and in which students learn to appreciate others by sharing in their successes.

Success, and the affirmation of it, creates an upward spiral that gives students a sense of growth, of improvement, of being worthwhile and capable. These characteristics, it seems to me, are essential to real academic achievement. Imagine a classroom in which every student has a high level of self-esteem; then imagine the heights to which that group could be taken. If you can envision that, you'll have had a glimpse of the world of the possible and your role in it.

# Twenty-five Ways Parents Can Help Kids Develop Self-esteem

No teacher can be optimally successful without enlisting the aid of parents. Children spend far more time with parents than they do at school, so the role of parents is even more important than that of teachers. Here are some things parents (and teachers too) can do with young children to build self-esteem and to prepare them for adolescence and adulthood.

1. **Let them do things to help, especially when they express a desire to do so.** Our four- and five-year-old daughters desperately wanted to help me paint the deck; so we covered them up with paint shirts, handed them brushes, and turned them loose. They made a hell of a mess, but they were actually successful in covering what they set out to paint. After a half-hour they were finished. We cleaned them up and they were elated as they sat, drank juice, and watched me finish the job. It would have been quicker, easier, and far less messy to do it myself, but by letting them help we increased the chances they'd offer to help again, or that they wouldn't balk if their mother or I asked them to do something.

   When kids help, be sure to thank them. Tell them how much their help means to the family (or the class), but avoid telling them that they have pleased you. If kids think their every act has to please mom or dad (or teacher), then they lose sight of the idea that we work not to please someone else, but for our own pleasure in doing the job.

2. **Praise and encourage them frequently, but make it specific to the act.** The accent is on building them up, so that their confidence and self-image develop along healthy lines. Praise needs to be sincere; so if you can't praise their "product," then perhaps you can praise their effort, their willingness to try, or their persistence in completing the task.

   In everything that a child does, try to find something to praise. If correction is necessary, and it will be, make it gentle, constructive, and positive. Adults often make the mistake of focusing a child's attention only on the errors made. If children repeatedly hear about their mistakes, two things happen: first, they become unable to recognize what they have done competently; and second, they become reluctant to try new things because of the criticism that will inevitably follow.

These children are easy to spot; they say things like "I got ten wrong on the spelling test" (rather than forty correct) or "I'm no good at math" (at the ripe old age of eight or nine). These children have learned to focus on their deficiencies rather than their competence. So adults can help by praising the positive, encouraging their effort, and convincing the children that it is the error that needs attention, not the children themselves. Separate the child from the act—and keep them separate.

3. **Avoid making a child an "approval-junkie."** These kids say things like "Is this good?", "Do you like this?", "Did I do well?", and other questions to generate approval from the adults in their lives. Kids who rely on external validation from key people when they are very young will continue to do so into adolescence and adulthood. And guess who the key people become in adolescence: their peer group.

When kids ask for your approval for something they have done, resist the urge to say things like "Yes, it's wonderful" or "Yes, I like it very much" or "You pleased me very much." Instead, turn the tables. Say: "What do *you* think about it?", "Tell me what *you* like about it," or "*You* must feel great about doing such a good job." Have the child himself determine the quality or competence of the job done. With time, the child will learn to evaluate his effort and results, no longer dependent on external validation. The child also becomes more able to accept criticism from others.

This is not to say that adults should ever withhold their approval. I have actually seen many adults who do withhold approval, not to make their children more independent and more self-reliant, but because they want their children to *earn* their approval, acceptance, or love. Nobody should have to *earn* these things; they must be given freely to every child. Affirm kids when they need it, but be careful about the words you use to do it.

4. **Create conditions that allow kids to make decisions.** Let kids decide on things that affect them from a very young age. For example, let them choose what they will wear and then suppress the overwhelming nausea you may feel at some of the combinations. They'll choose whatever makes them feel good or secure or happy.

Similarly, and this is tough, be aware that all but the youngest of kids are smart enough to know when they are too cold or too hot or too wet. Battling with them to do up their jackets against the winter chill is common where I live. Left long enough, they will make the right choice and, unless there is a serious threat of illness or injury, we have to let them decide.

As an example, I took my five-year-old camping one autumn weekend. After a blustery day on the lake we came back to camp about 7:00 p.m. It was cold and damp and we could see our breath. As I was rustling around getting supper, I noticed she had taken off her heavy coat to play with the children in the next campsite. Every cell in my body screamed that I should tell her to put her coat back on, that it was freezing, and that she would catch a cold. But I didn't. I wanted to see if she would make that decision for herself.

Ten interminable minutes later I looked up from the stove to see that she had not only put her coat on, but had done it up. I asked her why she had decided to put her coat on and she gave me the obvious answer "because I'm getting cold." Although I was anxious (How would I feel if I brought her home sick? What would her mother say?), to Molly it was no big deal: one minute she was playing and getting colder; the next minute she had put on her coat. She made a decision on her own, without me making it for her.

Obviously there are times when, for safety reasons or because kids are sometimes unable to anticipate negative consequences, decisions have to be made for them. Deciding what to wear today is not a safety issue; deciding whether to go swimming in the river is. If kids are given enough opportunities to make decisions when they are young, chances are that when they are older and it comes to a decision about swimming in the river, they'll make a wise one.

5. **Avoid nicknames or pet names that kids dislike.** As kids grow older they often come to hate the names hung on them when very small. This is particularly true when it comes to names that refer to a physical characteristic such as being overweight, very tall or short, or having some facial characteristic that stands out. If the name elicits a strong emotional response from the child, stop using it.

   Even worse are names that make reference to a child's intelligence or capability. A kid called Dummy or Stupid, even once, will quickly become convinced that it is true. Why shouldn't he? As the most important adults in your child's life, everything you say is understood to be true. Future performance will be inhibited because the child will feel that he is mentally inferior to others.

6. **Behave as though your child is capable (even when you suspect he isn't).** Adults sometimes make decisions for their kids based on whether or not they feel the kids are capable. Comments like "you're too young," "you're not big enough [strong enough, fast enough, tall enough, or smart enough]," "that's too hard for you," or "you'll understand when you're older" tell kids that they are somehow deficient. Like the speed with which unwanted nicknames are internalized, these messages shatter whatever feelings of confidence and self-worth the child may already possess, and he will spend much of his time saying "I can't, because I'm not...."

7. **Use reward systems sparingly, and never for meeting expectations over an unreasonably long period of time.** I am always a bit saddened when a youngster comes bounding up to me in September and says "If I do well in school this year, my dad's going to buy me a dirt bike!" or "If I get all A's on my report card, my dad's going to take us to Disneyland at spring break." The parents, while well meaning, are trying to motivate their children to do their best by offering big-ticket rewards

for doing pretty much what is expected of them anyway. Not only that, but chances are the kid will get the dirt bike or the Disneyland junket regardless of performance.

Reward systems deteriorate quickly for a number of reasons. One is that long-term goals, with the prize at the end, are interminably long for children, for whom a whole school year seems much as a decade seems to an adult. Kids lose sight of the purpose of the reward and focus instead on the end result. Another problem is that the motivation undergoes a drastic shift: high performance becomes tied to the expectation of future tangible gain, rather than to the expectation of learning and growing. Thus, the motivation is based externally rather than internally, when the whole point of the exercise is for the child to learn to become self-motivated.

Another problem is the "cash for A's" syndrome, with kids offered cash rewards for A grades. This creates two absolutely false values: first, the whole reason we work hard is for monetary gain; and second, anything less than perfect is not worthy of reward. Little wonder then that when the reward system is terminated, there is no real change in the behavior of the child; there is no incentive for him to improve because "there's nothing in it for me." This attitude frequently survives into adulthood. How many adults have you met in your life who approach everything from the point of view of what could be in it for them? Perhaps they were rewarded for all the wrong things.

Some experts suggest that any rewards should consist of time spent with the family doing special things, not of money or gifts. This is a good idea as far as it goes, but beware the negative consequence if the child does not meet the expectation. Does that mean that if he doesn't make the grade, we should withdraw that time? No, of course not. Besides, you don't want to fall into the trap of tying family time spent doing enjoyable things to performance. So, tread softly with this idea.

The whole concept of offering rewards for changes in behavior is a hotly debated issue. If you can find a reward system that actually results in a permanent behavioral change, then use it. Usually though, rewards are successful only in modifying behavior for the period of time during which the system is in place, and the weaning from rewards can be painful for all concerned.

8. **Parents should insist on time spent together as a family.** This includes mealtimes and is increasingly difficult to achieve when everyone in the house has different schedules of work, meetings, clubs, sports, and so on. Family time also includes day outings and vacations. Some require detailed planning, but most do not. Even gathering the whole group to watch a favorite movie or TV program can help maintain a sense of family togetherness.

It is important for families to develop their own traditions concerning special days like Christmas and Easter (or whichever religious holidays your family observes) as well as birthdays. Families also need to create their own rituals and legends—special things that belong to the family and nobody else. And every family member must understand that "this is the way our family does things." When adult siblings sit down and begin reminiscing about the pleasant and humorous experiences they had at home as children, they are speaking of the legends, rituals, and traditions they grew up with. Building those same things in our own families is crucial to strengthening feelings of acceptance, belonging, and safety in our children.

As an example: Friends of ours were able, with much scrimping and saving, to take a year's leave of absence from their jobs. They spent twelve weeks traveling in Asia with their thirteen- and fifteen-year-old daughters. The single most positive result of the trip, according to both parents, was the strengthening of family bonds, between and among all members. When you have only the family to rely on, they reported, your survival depends on family cohesion. At the same time, their shared memories of the trip helped strengthen their already strong family traditions, rituals, and legends.

While not everyone can afford twelve weeks in Asia, the same family ethic can be developed in everyday life.

The trick is to focus on family values and time spent together. In the eighties, a number of workaholic so-called yuppies talked about "budgeting quality time" with their kids. Here's some news for those people: *any* time spent with your children is quality time.

9. **Show, don't tell.** Most people learn to do by doing, not by being told how. Kids learning to perform manual tasks will make mistakes and must be allowed to make them without being criticized. The child who wants to "help" you take the carburetor apart, or prepare dinner, or rake the leaves, or any number of other household tasks will learn better if allowed to try and, perhaps, allowed to fail. Most kids are naturally curious about how things work and how to do things, so it is important to capture their interest by allowing them to try.

Becoming impatient and frustrated with a child when he's messing up is probably natural, but to say "it's easier to do it myself" guarantees two outcomes: first, the child isn't apt to try whatever it is again; and second, the adult will end up doing it all the time, even when the child grows older and more capable. The adult who complains that the kid won't cut the lawn may be the same parent who took the mower away from the kid when he was five or six because he couldn't cut a straight line.

10. **Don't associate making a mistake with degree of personal worth.** Many adults—men far more than women—are afraid of making any kind of mistake in front of their kids. Men are still socialized to be strong, invulnerable, and in control, three factors that suggest that making mistakes threatens the ways in which others view them as men. Parents think they will lose their children's respect if they mess up, so they either deny their mistake ("No, it wasn't *my* mistake") or try to lay the blame on someone or something else ("I was late only because the neighbor didn't tell me what time it was"). Unfortunately, adults who behave this way use the wrong approach.

Recalling that our children will model our behavior, what message will they receive if we don't take responsibility for our mistakes, or if we blame other people when we mess up? These children will learn only that to admit an error is bad, which implies that mistakes themselves are unacceptable and committed only by someone else. Kids need to see adults not only making errors, but admitting them and taking responsibility for the consequences. Kids whose parents (and teachers) never acknowledge mistakes will seldom acknowledge them either, and this will become even truer in adolescence.

11. **Never underestimate the power of a simple apology.** Nobody, whether a child, adolescent, or adult, is perfect. We all say and do things that hurt others, usually without meaning to and just as often without actually knowing it. Still, many adults (again, more men than women) have great difficulty telling a child they are sorry. This is related to adults not wanting to be seen by children as capable of making mistakes.

    The simple words "I'm sorry" give kids the message that you have understood that you have hurt them; that apologizing is not only all right, but necessary; and that when we hurt someone, we need to acknowledge it and make at least a gesture of reconciliation. "I'm sorry" will also defuse a vast number of conflicts with adolescents. Besides, what can you possibly say to someone who apologizes to you except "thanks," however grudgingly?

12. **Don't get hung up on the words kids use to provoke you.** They'll inevitably be angry when they are not permitted to do certain things, and they'll react verbally. They'll make broad, sweeping generalizations and will paint all parents (or teachers) with the same brush (in much the same way as adults will paint all adolescents). Don't buy into the language, the words, or the anger. Listen not so much to *what* they are saying, but *why* they might be saying it.

    Acknowledge that they are upset. Empathize if you can. Confirm that you know they are angry and ask if they can tell you why. Be calm, be patient, be non-confrontational. Don't escalate the conflict by responding with aggression. *Don't take the bait.* Remember that you are the adult here. The last thing you want to do is to draw lines in the sand and dare them to cross, or issue ultimatums like "my way or the highway." Too many kids have chosen the highway, and with heartbreaking results.

13. **Establish and maintain productive contact with the school (or, if you are a teacher, with the home).** Take an interest in your child's schooling by establishing a cooperative working relationship with the teacher and principal. Children who know that their teachers and parents are in regular contact are less prone to try to play two ends against the middle. Also, while kids' personalities are essentially the same at school and at home, there is often a marked difference in behavior. The child who is quiet and compliant at home may be victimized or ostracized at school. Frequent home-school communication can identify far more than academic concerns.

    There will be times when teachers and parents are at odds about any number of issues, often related to the consequences of behavior; however, ultimately they both want the same thing—a happy, adjusted child who is achieving at a level appropriate to his ability. It is therefore critical that positive relationships be established between home and school.

14. **Ask your child open-ended questions.** Open-ended questions are those designed to elicit more than a one-word response. They require the child to think and to come up with an answer. The opposite are closed-ended questions. These can be answered with a single word, or, all too frequently, with "I don't know." Every parent has probably asked the question "What did you learn in school today?" and has been given the answer "Nothing." A prime example of misuse of closed-ended questions can be witnessed when TV news reporters interview small children. Interviewers tend to ask children questions that elicit yes, no, good, I don't know, and other less-than-exhilarating answers.

    Instead of closed-ended questions like "Did you like that?", try "Tell me what you liked about that." Instead of "What did you learn in school today?", try "What are you working on in math right now?" or "What do you like about the novel you are reading?" Open-ended questions help children articulate their thoughts and give them practice recalling information.

15. **Monitor television and video watching closely.** Some parents sidestep this issue by simply not having a television set, or forbidding its use. This doesn't really deal with the issue at all, but merely avoids it. Kids who can't watch TV at home will develop elaborate strategies to watch it elsewhere, usually with little or no supervision at all.

    Watch TV *with* your kids, talk about what you're watching (the annoying frequency of commercials guarantees plenty of discussion time), and set clear guidelines about what is and isn't acceptable *and why.* If you are concerned about the violence, sexism, and racism that are represented on Saturday morning cartoons, say so when you forbid them.

    Similarly, don't put a rented movie on for the kids without previewing it. Many a parent has been appalled by what another parent has recommended as suitable for viewing, finding it unacceptably violent or otherwise inappropriate. Of course, this only seems to happen when the neighbor's kids are over, and they go home to tell mommy what they saw at your place!

16. **Stress that we never make fun of anyone.** Kids who frequently see and hear adults making fun of or ridiculing others will model that behavior. This has two negative effects: first, it sets them up for serious conflict when the object of ridicule decides to retaliate; and second, it teaches them to look for the weaknesses or deficiencies in other people and to exploit them from a distorted sense of what is funny. This will be covered in detail in chapter four.

17. **Don't allow kids' bedrooms to become fortresses.** More and more adolescents have rooms that are nearly self-sufficient. Some kids' rooms have TVs, VCRs, video games, stereo systems, and telephones. Other than to eat and use the bathroom, what possible incentive is there for kids with these kinds of rooms to leave them?

If these kids are allowed to withdraw, they will—even more so at the onset of adolescence.

Kids who spend too much time alone can become incredibly self-absorbed and remote from the family. If they are experiencing anxiety or depression about issues involving their peers, and are allowed to withdraw into the safety of Fortress Bedroom, they won't be able to communicate with their parents or siblings. Instead they will probably spend hours on the phone with similarly confused and like-minded peers, reinforcing their own insecurities and quite possibly badly distorting reality.

18. **Give serious consideration to a children's phone line.** At adolescence, kids feel a natural need to speak with their friends more frequently and for longer, sometimes interminable, periods of time. Phone access causes countless arguments in households where parents need access to the phone too. If you choose to solve the problem by installing a separate phone line for the kids, establish the following guidelines: first, the phone will be in a "public" area of the house, not in a bedroom; second, the kids will pay for the installation and monthly bills.

    The first guideline is aimed at discouraging kids' withdrawal for extended periods; the second gives them responsibility. They'll be dumbfounded if the phone is cut off because they've forgotten to pay the bill. If you choose not to install a separate phone line, then don't be surprised if your kids spend more time away from home, making their calls from a pay phone at the corner convenience store.

19. **Consider having only one television set and negotiating its use.** Sure, you can probably afford an inexpensive second TV, but as soon as you add one, you open up the household to the formation of alliances. Though this is admittedly a minor issue, the negotiation of what we will watch in the next two hours teaches the value of give-and-take. This will only work, of course, if parents are willing to sit through a few things they absolutely hate.

One family I know had, at one time, three teenagers, each with decidedly different tastes in TV. They negotiated a regime in which each day one person in the family had absolute control over the remote channel changer. It took some time, but eventually everyone was satisfied with the arrangement, so much so that even when one was away for the evening, the rest watched the shows that the absent one would have chosen.

20. **Foster compassion and awareness of those less fortunate than yourself.** Let your kids see you donating money, serviceable used clothing, and household goods to charitable agencies. Let them observe you doing volunteer work in your local community or at a school. If we want our kids to develop social awareness and compassion for others, we have to model it.

21. **Make your home a haven for your kids and their friends.** Sure, furniture costs money and cleaning carpets costs a lot too, but it's better if the kids and their friends mess up your house than wander aimlessly in the streets looking for fun. And those things that start out as innocent fun often result in an unwelcome lift home by a police officer. Yes, parents work hard in the decorating and upkeep of their homes, but if that becomes more important than offering a safe place for kids and their friends, there's a problem. Besides, kids who feel free to bring their friends home when they are six will probably continue to do so when they are sixteen, when you *really* want to keep your finger on the pulse.

22. **Give kids a sense of "doing the right thing."** Often, the right thing is the difficult thing. To say you are sorry, to admit that you broke something or that you were careless is only a small part. The really important issues are the ethical and moral ones. Demonstrate to your kids that you will do the right thing, even when you don't want to or when the results may well be unpleasant.

When they get their first jobs, kids will often be tempted to call in sick on a Saturday night so that they can go to the social gathering they've been looking forward to for months. As a parent, if you let them do it, you are giving your approval for them to do the wrong thing. If you insist that they go to work, you risk their ire, but they will have learned a lesson about ethics and morals. Allowing kids the easy way out of their obligations only ensures that they'll continue to take the easy route, and when the stakes are much higher, you'd like to know that they'll make the right choice, no matter how hard it may be.

23. **Invite kids to select an appropriate consequence for their misdeeds.** How much more effective it is if the kid decides his transgression is worth a two-week grounding than if the parent decides it. Make clear the expectations for behavior and the consequences for noncompliance. Stress that you have no choice in the matter, that by choosing to behave thus and so, then this is the consequence that applies.

    Lead children to understand that behavior is a conscious decision, and deciding to do something, despite the known consequences is an acceptance of the inevitability of the consequence. As a parent, your job is simply to see that the consequence is applied. Parents who assume the role of judge, jury, and executioner take responsibility for their child's actions on their own shoulders and set themselves up as evil villains on whom the child can direct his anger and resentment. What we want is for the kid to accept personal responsibility, and he can't do that if you, the parent, are to blame for his one-month grounding.

24. **Increase the odds that your kids will respect you by respecting them.** This involves virtually everything discussed so far in this chapter. Speak with respect, without demeaning or devaluing them. Give them credit for making decisions and choices. Reinforce their behaviors that benefit them, not you. Trust their judgments and soften the urge to be overly critical and corrective. Respect cannot be demanded, nor is it something that all children automatically owe all adults because of their age. We must start from an assumption of respect and then modify from there if it is proven that

respect is premature. It is possible to lose respect, but it is also possible to regain it.

25. **Trust your kids.** With very rare exceptions, children are trustworthy. I have never encountered a young child who deliberately set out to do things that would result in a loss of trust by the key adults in his life. This is because, like respect, kids begin with the assumption that they are trusted by their parents. It is only later, when faced with suspicion, accusation, and constant reminders about their transgressions, that they begin to play by the "give me the name and I'll play the game" routine.

So, parents, trust your kids. Make your love for them known and make it unconditional. If you have worked hard to help them develop into responsible, moral, ethical, thoughtful individuals who can make decisions and solve problems, they will not disappoint. Instead they will become better able to survive and to flourish in our complicated world. In the end, that's the very least we can hope for.

## To Bottle the Wind

Helping children develop healthy levels of self-esteem is painstakingly difficult, requiring constant vigilance from practically the moment they are born until the moment they leave their family homes to make their own ways in the world. If parents and teachers are always aware of the importance of having a practical, optimistic, and humane mind-set; of the incredible power of strong role modeling; and of using positive methods for building self-esteem, we should enjoy at least some measure of success with the children in our lives. Similarly, the whole concept of building a healthy environment cannot be overstressed. Self-esteem is not a destination, but a journey fraught with enormous pitfalls. With the help of caring, understanding adults, our children will be well served, and just may fulfill the dreams that we have for them and, even more important, the dreams they have for themselves.

# Peer Pressure:
# More Powerful Than a Locomotive

## About Tasha

*I heard Tasha coming before I actually saw her. The friendly grade-six girl literally sobbed her way down the hall and straight into my office. She'd simply got up and left her classroom following yet another bout of teasing. It wasn't even a major incident this time; two girls had made a point of making sure she saw them whispering behind their hands, smiling, laughing, and pointing at her. This time she'd had enough, so she walked out to the muted jeers and laughs of her classmates and to the utter bewilderment of her teacher, who was occupied with a small group in a corner of the classroom.*

*In the refuge of my office, she poured out her heart. It didn't matter* WHAT *she did, the kids still bugged her constantly. She had a high-pitched, little-girl voice that the others found easy to mimic. Tasha was a creative thinker whose ideas could well be considered a little far out from time to time, and the other kids couldn't wait to pounce on her more unconventional ideas. It is unfair, though, to say "the other kids"; it was really only two or three of the most popular girls who had decided that Tasha was to be the whipping girl. The other girls were too timid to stand up to them, so joined in to avoid becoming the victims of such abuse themselves.*

*This, in essence, is the crux of peer influence, or peer pressure. Kids in groups will go along with all manner of cruel-ties, not so much because of any legitimate enmity for the victim, but for fear of being different, of standing up or standing out, and therefore running a greater risk of being ostracized, bullied, taunted, and abused themselves. When I went into the class and very quietly but firmly stated that enough was enough, there were only one or two smirks and a couple of dozen sheepish expressions. My message was simple and direct: Lay off or deal with me. I sometimes have to do this, though I wish I didn't.*

*Tasha was really quite a delightful kid who was kind to younger kids, thoughtful in her dealings with her classmates, and a talented writer and performer. Why, then, was she treated so badly? Simply put, she was different, and since kids at that age don't like DIFFERENT, they attack. The result is great unhappiness for the attacked; all sorts of negative results can accrue for that person. In Tasha's case, though, she blew her nose, dried her tears, squared her shoulders, and headed once more into the breach. I admired her courage and perseverance.*

*Tasha made it through the rest of grade six and all of grade seven with only a few problems. The kids didn't change their approach, but Tasha herself learned to cope by having, as she told me, belief in herself and her abilities. She'd found a way to ignore most of the taunts and, by the time she went to high school, she actually seemed relatively happy. But kids like Tasha are rare; all too often they crash and burn, and few of their peers are willing to stay around and help pick up the pieces. And all of it, it appears, is a result of that more-powerful-than-a-locomotive peer pressure.*

If teachers and parents have one overwhelming worry as their children march inevitably toward adolescence, it is the fear of a whole set of complex social interactions that fall under the convenient heading of peer pressure. Included within this broad concept are the major adult fears of drugs, alcohol, and sexual activity that results in pregnancy or a sexually transmitted disease.

Peer pressure is also blamed for the increasing lack of power and control that parents begin to feel as their children approach the teenage years. All of a sudden the happy, compliant child who could be counted on to conform with their every wish now fights and argues at every turn and begins to isolate himself from the rest of the family. Faced with such massive changes, parents begin to look outside the home for reasons for this behavior and latch onto the notion of peer pressure as being largely responsible.

Parents find themselves telling their children that they don't really have to be like everyone else, that they don't have to wear the same clothes, adopt the same hairstyles, use the same language and tone of voice, or advocate the same values as their friends. Sadly, they miss the point; the very last thing pre- and early adolescent children want to be is different. They do not want to stand out. They do not want to be different, because to be different is to be wrong, and to be wrong is to invite correction from those who are right. And, when peer group leaders dispense correction, it is frequently brutal and unfeeling, using ridicule, ostracism, and sometimes even physical abuse.

Peer group leaders are neither elected nor selected, but everyone knows who they are. Some are keenly aware of the social power that comes with being viewed as a leader and develop a sizable constituency. To maintain their popularity, they must fulfill a role not entirely of their own making, that of the quasi-official arbiter of everything from fashion to language to spare-time pursuits to attitudes toward peers, adults, and authority in general. Most children, especially those possessing even a little uncertainty, shaky self-esteem, or outright fear are more than willing to keep their mouths shut and do whatever is necessary to fit in.

The obvious questions that parents, teachers, and administrators need to find the answers for involve those that ask "Why is peer pressure so powerful?", "What factors make our children so vulnerable to it?", and "What can we do to prepare our children for their overwhelming need to fit in?" Staggeringly complex questions all, but it is worth the effort to try to answer them to understand what peer pressure is and what it does.

## What Is Peer Pressure?

The following is a useful definition of peer pressure, or peer influence: *the normally unspoken pressure kids feel to think and behave in ways their peers do.* Though somewhat discredited by some modern academics, Abraham Maslow years ago developed a hierarchy of needs that all human beings possess. The most basic of needs is simple survival in the form of food, shelter, clothing, air to breathe, and water to drink. The most complex need is for what Maslow terms "self-actualization," a level on which we are finally equipped to meet our own needs, where we no longer require outside affirmation for who or what we are.

In the middle of Maslow's hierarchy are the needs for safety, for belonging, and for acceptance. Until early adolescence, kids can pretty much count on parents and the school to meet their needs for personal safety, whether physical, emotional, or psychological. Parents and teachers are largely successful in controlling the child's environment in such a way that major threats to safety are at least minimized.

Similarly, and because pre-adolescent children are generally compliant and will normally defer to adult authority, the need for acceptance is also met. In terms of belonging, pre-adolescence is a time when families tend to be the most cohesive, simply because adults generally decide what is going to happen, what their children are to do, and when they are to do it. Elementary classes stay together as groups, sometimes for several years in succession, thereby making the need for belonging less of an issue.

Now, fast-forward to the first year of high school. All of a sudden, children go from the relative security of a small intermediate school to a substantially larger high school, where they are the youngest and smallest, where they may not even see the friends they grew up with, and where older students are perceived as a threat, sometimes with ample reason. Emotional, psychological, and physical safety become very real issues, particularly in the minds of those lacking high levels of confidence and self-esteem.

The sense of belonging begins to evaporate, since old friends begin to form new friendships and alliances, and since early high school does not particularly lend itself to a kid's sense of belonging on a broad level. The need for acceptance is probably greater than ever, but kids begin to look for it outside the classroom, where teachers cannot realistically hope to develop meaningful relationships with each of the 150 students they see each day. And kids search for acceptance outside the home, where they feel that their parents are trying to control their every thought and move. Acceptance from peers becomes a high priority in their lives.

In over twenty years of working with pre- and early adolescent children, I have found that elementary children, up until grade six or seven, consider parents, teachers, and peers to be the most influential people in their lives—in that order. By early adolescence the peer group rockets into the lead, with parents and teachers a very distant second and third. There are all kinds of reasons why this seems to be so for most kids. But before discussing those reasons, let's break down peer pressure into its various types.

✦ **Overt peer pressure.** Overt peer pressure is the kind that usually comes to mind when the term *peer pressure* is used. Overt peer pressure is that which dares, challenges, or orders someone to do something. "Come on, have a beer. Everyone else is drinking" or "What's the matter? You afraid to do it?" Kids using this type of peer pressure always use direct *do* statements, and the message is clear: If you do it (whatever "it" is), you'll fit in. The needs for acceptance and belonging are met, despite the fact that the kid's own judgment tells him it may not be safe or smart.

Failure to give in to overt peer pressure opens the kid up to all kinds of unpleasant consequences. Sarcasm that belittles, loud ridicule, teasing, taunting, and the possibility of physical abuse are common devices used by peer group leaders to make others fall into line, thereby increasing their own power base. While this is the type of peer pressure with which everyone can readily identify, it is often the easiest to deal with since it is so out in the open. Kids learn quickly how to construct elaborate avoidance strategies.

✦ **Covert peer pressure.** A much more slippery concept, covert peer pressure is virtually always unspoken and grounded in kids' beliefs about how to think, how to behave, how to dress, and how to talk. These beliefs are formed by watching and emulating others, seeing what works for others and what doesn't. Sometimes kids are told what is and isn't cool or acceptable, and they add this information to the beliefs they are forming about how to be safe, to belong, and to be accepted. Examples of this kind of thinking can be heard when kids say things like "Well, everyone does it that way," or "Everyone will think I'm out of it if I don't." Sadly, these kids make assumptions about what other people are thinking about them, then try to tailor their behavior to meet those perceived thoughts.

✦ **Silent-consent peer pressure.** An aspect of covert peer pressure, silent consent results from the fear of speaking up when something wrong—often something unspeakably cruel—is being done to another peer. It is predictable that within every large group of kids, at least one will be singled out to be the victim of all manner of abuse. As adults, we can all remember someone like that from our own school days, or perhaps one of our own children was, or is, that child. Peers may vehemently disagree with the way others are treated, but remain silent out of fear that they might become the next victims. By way of example, the following is an account of just such a boy from my own high school experience over twenty-five years ago.

*To say that I went to school with Alan is misleading; we went to the same large Vancouver high school. Other than that we had little contact. Thinking back with the wisdom that accrues with hindsight, I realize that Alan, who didn't have a father, didn't have much money either. He was an odd-looking boy, with an unusually large forehead and thick glasses. He wore the same clothes almost all the time, which was naturally unacceptable to the student fashion arbiters that exist in every school. He was friendless and an easy target for all those middle-echelon bullies looking for another trophy on their way to major-league status.*

*In the school's cafeteria, bottles of pop were sold, and in those days a returned empty was worth two cents. High-school students then, as now, would rather have kissed a Rottweiler full on the lips than turn in a bottle for pennies. Alan had no such compunction. Every noon hour he would circulate through the cafeteria, picking up discarded bottles to make enough money to eat. His tormentors would commit all manner of atrocities on the bottles: spitting on the necks, smearing them with peanut butter and mayonnaise, stuffing everything they* could think of into the bottles. Some bottles were tossed into garbage cans, just to watch Alan have to suffer the indignity of pawing through half-eaten food remains to get them. Later, Alan would sit alone, off in some corner, trying as hard as he could to ignore the testosterone-fueled taunts and jeers of his schoolmates. He'd learned very early to maintain an impassive expression in the face of incessant verbal barbs.

This continued all through the school year, until Alan didn't show up for school one day, or the next day, or any day after that. Alan had gone into his room one night and had hanged himself in his closet.

At school there was a momentary hush as word spread across the cafeteria like a fog. The hush gave way to that peculiar brand of teenaged gallows humor that was nothing more than a collectively inept attempt to make light of tragic consequences. Some of us actually felt badly about Alan, but none dared say so. Even his death didn't appear to have changed anything.

In the end—though there may have been other factors unrelated to school—Alan died because none of us had the courage to do anything but watch a clearly reluctant fighter become cut and bruised on the outside, battered and shattered on the inside. None of us wanted to be different, to stand up or stand out, for fear of suffering Alan's fate. When Alan died, a part of all of us who knew him died too, and that part was our innocence of the power of the mob. We all learned a hard lesson about the tragedy that can result from teasing the weak, the vulnerable, and the visibly different.

There is no doubt that all three types of peer pressure—overt, covert, and silent consent—are difficult to come to terms with. Resisting overt peer pressure runs the risk of ostracism, which can last for months and years. Resisting covert peer pressure generates pretty much the same results. Silent consent is particularly difficult to resist, because it asks the student to step out of his self-created safety net to challenge peer group leaders, thereby risking acceptance and belonging—and probably becoming the odds-on favorite for victim of the week, month, or year.

## Why Are Kids So Vulnerable to Peer Pressure?

Parents and teachers tear their graying hair out, wondering whatever happened to that sweet happy child who has suddenly become so incredibly difficult. They desperately try to figure out what the allure of the peer group might be, that it could lead to such troublesome changes. Maybe the following ideas will help.

✦ **Adolescents are no longer children and no longer want to have their every move controlled.** They want more control over their lives; they want to make decisions about what they will wear, what they think, and with whom they'll associate. If we raise our kids to be independent thinkers, then we'd better be prepared to accept their need to stretch their wings. Too often, we have it completely backward: we give them all kinds of choices and freedoms when they are very young, but begin to restrict them more when they reach late elementary and high school age, just when they feel the need to venture out into the world.

✦ **Adolescents very much need to feel as though they belong and to be accepted as part of the group.** As adolescence approaches, just being a member of a family no longer meets all of an adolescent's need to belong. This is a time when new interests form: music, movies, sports, dating, academic or vocational pursuits. Often, belonging to a group of peers meets those needs, as long as it is socially acceptable to the greater group. Parents and teachers who keep their kids actively engaged can help them with this if they can manage to capture their interest in something they enjoy and in which they are surrounded by like-minded individuals.

✦ **Adolescents want to have their beliefs and values validated through the parallel experiences of their peers.** The notion that misery loves company is especially apropos here. All kids talk about the real and imagined injustices they suffer at the hands of parents, teachers, and the school. Finding out that other kids fight the same battles with the adults in their lives gives them a sense of belonging, albeit in a negative way. A number of adolescent truisms become articulated and reinforced, such as "They don't want me to have any fun" or "They don't trust me." Still, it's natural and normal.

- ✦ **Adolescents become acutely aware of the inconsistencies in the behavior of the adults in their lives.** They tend to see almost any issue in terms of black and white; inexperience with the world-at-large has yet to teach them the wisdom of seeing gray where it exists. Thus adolescents become almost obsessive about what is fair and what is not. Telling them "life isn't fair" only reinforces what they already fervently believe. Instead they view that statement, and rightly so in my opinion, as just another way adults say "shut up."

- ✦ **Adolescents see liberation from adult control in the class rebels and clowns.** In a sense, many kids see the deliberate rule-breakers—the smokers, the drinkers, the ones who recklessly drive fast cars—as kinds of role models. These are the ones who have fought back by not complying. Class clowns fall into the same category. I usually advise teachers never to get into a power struggle with the class clown: his constituency is larger than yours.

- ✦ **Gratification of pleasure urges becomes more complex at adolescence.** Adolescents are no longer satisfied with childhood pastimes, one reason why parents sometimes find it a battle to coax the adolescent child into yet another summer at the lake. To parents it's paradise; to the kid it has become Devil's Island. Adult pastimes begin to have more allure; so it is not unusual for kids at this age to experiment with alcohol, tobacco, drugs, and sex. Parents can help by talking openly about these things instead of threatening death or dismemberment for any kid who even thinks about them.

- ✦ **Adolescents want to carve out their own individual niche, but they often don't know how.** Their formerly held values about doing well in school and being obedient sons or daughters pale in the face of contrary values held by the peer group. It becomes easier to follow the herd, from which they take their cues and from which feedback is immediate and clear—sometimes even corrective. If following lessens their anxiety, then no amount of advice to the contrary will prevent them from doing so.

For many kids, following is the only way to survive. If resisting peer pressure or influence results in continual verbal, psycho-emotional or physical abuse, then they internalize the belief that it is easier to follow. Parents have a tough time with this, because they are uncertain of the extent to which their children will go to fit in, and they fear the worst. Well-known Colorado educator Barbara Coloroso advises parents that if it isn't immoral, illegal, or life-threatening, then hush up. The trick is raising them from an early age to recognize "immoral, illegal, and life-threatening" and to know how to pull the ripcord when one or more of those factors is present.

## How Do Adolescents Cope with Peer Pressure?

For the most part, adolescents tend to deal with peer pressure and peer influence by adopting one of several coping mechanisms, some positive and constructive, others quite the opposite.

There are many adolescents who, because of their own healthy level of self-esteem, their long-standing acceptance in a group of like-minded friends, and their open communication with the important adults in their lives, can survive quite ably in the face of peer pressure. This group is a distinct minority. Most adolescents adopt one or more of the following coping mechanisms:

✦ **They follow enthusiastically.** These kids find freedom from adult control and revel in it. They are delighted to interpret what teachers and parents call *personal responsibility* as freedom to do nothing at all if they wish. This sometimes results in these kids deceiving, lying, and blaming others for the unpleasant consequences that inevitably accrue. Sneaking out, staying out past curfew, telling his parents baldfaced lies about where he was, who he was with, and what he was doing are indicators of the enthusiastic follower. Some kids revel in being admired by others for their audacity and get an ego-boost by being affirmed by their peers. These kids aren't bad kids, just misled and unable to see the future consequences of their actions.

How do kids get this way? Perhaps these are the kids who have never had to make choices or decisions, or whose lives were largely controlled by adults since birth. Perhaps they were never made to be accountable, or were let off the hook so many times when they failed to comply that they know how to spot the weakness in any coat of armor and how to exploit it. Either way, we must never assume that these kids are not intelligent enough to know better; often they are among the brightest. This is what makes them all the more perplexing to their parents and teachers.

+ **They follow quietly for fear of becoming victims.** This is a potentially dangerous group, in the sense that they are easily influenced, unassertive, silent in the face of cruelty toward others, and will not report others' criminal activity. They don't mind being led; it is easy and hassle-free. Kids in this group often sacrifice their own beliefs and values in an attempt to ally themselves with peer leaders. They do so to achieve peer status, thereby increasing their self-esteem.

+ **They withdraw and become loners.** These kids, because they so obviously do not fit in, inevitably become the object of scorn and ridicule. There are two main subgroups here: those with sufficient strength of character to withstand it and those who become so withdrawn that they are often at serious risk of self-harm, up to and including suicide. This second subgroup is frightening in the extreme, because these kids are often unwilling or unable to communicate their pain.

+ **They seek out a peer group where safety in numbers affords protection.** Many times these are groups based outside of school, including church groups, Scouts, Guides, Cadets, drama or dance groups, clubs, service groups, sports groups, or others. The need for acceptance, belonging, and safety are all met in such subgroups. Unfortunately, gangs provide precisely the same things but in a negative sense. Well-intentioned efforts to eliminate gangs will not succeed until their members' needs for safety, acceptance, and belonging are met in other positive ways.

◆ **They drop out or transfer to another school.** The escape tactic sometimes works, but just as often does not. If a kid obviously does not fit into one school, odds are that he won't fit in the next one either. An unsuccessful move will make the student more miserable than ever, and at greater risk of withdrawal. Besides, using escapism as a tactic does not help the escapee deal with the problem; it affirms the power of the peer group leaders, and it underscores the perceived need for everyone else to yield to the group.

◆ **They camouflage themselves.** These kids just try to be invisible, using a strategy I call the blue grouse tactic. The area in which I live is dissected by scores of gravel logging roads. In the fall it is possible to drive these roads hunting for blue grouse. When approached by a predator, the grouse adopts the only evasive action it knows, which is to stand absolutely motionless, hoping its mottled plumage will make it invisible. Any hunter who manages to spot one can simply take his time, aim and fire, and the grouse becomes dinner.

In the forest, in the absence of roads, this strategy has allowed the grouse to survive and flourish, but as humans have invaded the wilderness, the grouse hasn't adapted. Using the blue grouse tactic, some kids are largely ambivalent toward what is going on around them. They just want to be left alone, to stand motionless, and to blend into the scenery. Sooner or later, like the grouse, they are noticed, and the results are just as often unpleasant.

## How Can Teachers Help Kids Deal with Peer Pressure?

So now that we have a sense of what peer pressure is, what forms it takes, what makes kids so vulnerable to influence from peers, and what coping mechanisms they adopt, the big question is: what can parents, teachers, and administrators do to soften the impact of peer pressure, particularly among pre- and early adolescents? There are no instant solutions, no magic incantations or secret potions that, when sprinkled on kids' morning cornflakes, will guarantee overnight changes. Vulnerability to peer influence has taken years to develop.

What follows is an exploration of what teachers can do to help students deal with issues of peer pressure. While all of it is directed at teachers, it is equally applicable to principals, though from a slightly different perspective. The teacher is mostly concerned with the micro-climate of the classroom, while the principal is more concerned with the macro-climate of the school as a whole. While the teacher effects change at the classroom level, the principal attempts to effect change at the classroom level through the leadership of his teachers. Thus, the concepts and practices are essentially the same.

On the surface, it may appear to teachers that peer pressure is an issue that falls pretty much outside the framework of their responsibilities. How kids relate to each other and how they fit within the pecking order are seen by many teachers as beyond their control. In many cases this is true, but in many others it is not. If teachers are to help kids deal with peer pressure, there are things that can be done through formal instruction and, informally, during what teachers term "teachable moments."

Before we go any further, I can already hear an anguished chorus coming from staff rooms all over the land. It sounds like this: "You mean, on top of everything else we have to do, now you want us to teach kids how to deal with peer pressure?" Having been an educator for many, many years, I am painfully aware of the profoundly increased demands on teachers during that time. The good news, however, is that very little of the following asks teachers to use a direct instructional approach. Most of it consists of creating an environment conducive to positive relationships between and among students, and if that is done well enough, teachers can probably get by with minimal direct instruction.

How teachers deal with issues of peer pressure depends on a number of factors, including how we conceptualize the purposes and goals of education, how best to achieve those goals, and how we view the issues that either help or hinder the educational process.

The traditional concept of education was of a process that taught basic literacy and numeracy skills to obedient students so they could take their place as laborers in a resource-based, industrial society. Massive technological change, automation, and a greater need for service-oriented labor have shifted the focus dramatically. Now we want to produce students with strong communication and thinking skills, interpersonal and technological skills, flexibility, and the ability to solve complex problems and to work cooperatively with others. The traditional approach has become an albatross around the neck of education.

Arguments over methodologies ebb and flow depending upon whichever experts currently have the attention of the policy-makers. One thing seems abundantly clear: there is far more to education than the simple transmission of skills from one person to another, particularly when technological skills are intensifying and diversifying faster than anyone can keep up. So, a traditional, skill-based curriculum and its simplistic methodologies are outmoded.

The issues that affect society-at-large also affect our students. Children subject to poverty, transience, alcoholism, family disintegration, drug abuse, physical and sexual abuse, and neglect exist in virtually every school, and their needs, beyond academic ones, are too great to ignore. This leads us to the view of the teacher as an instructor-cum-social-worker, which is a truer representation of what teaching today is all about than the old-fashioned notion of teacher as firm-but-kindly school marm. Clearly, teachers are being called upon to respond with nontraditional strategies to educate nontraditional students.

Yes, teachers are constrained by time, resources, the number and degree of difficult behavior problems, the integration of special needs students into regular classrooms, and an ever-changing curriculum. The best hope is to create a safe environment, where a sense of acceptance and belonging flourishes and where difficult issues are dealt with openly, even when this means missing an occasional math drill, spelling test, or social studies class.

## Create a Safe, Accepting Classroom Environment

Teachers are keenly aware of the need to "set the tone" in their classrooms at the start of each new school year. This traditionally consisted of laying down the law; making sure the kids knew who the boss was; establishing a clear, restrictive code of classroom conduct, routines for work completion, and lists of consequences for noncompliance. Setting the tone involved letting kids know what they couldn't do and what they could expect if they didn't comply. In former, less complicated times, this traditional approach served the purpose. Little thought and effort went into creating a supportive learning environment.

To create a more supportive learning environment, setting the tone is still important, but from a more positive, constructive point of view, one that shows both an awareness and understanding of the problems faced by students and a willingness to address them.

There should be some guidelines about the way to behave in class. Though discussed in detail in chapter two, it is worthwhile to refer once again to the following basic understandings:

No one should be subjected to unwelcome teasing.

No one should laugh at the mistakes of others.

No one should be ridiculed for their beliefs or opinions, or their choices in clothing or footwear.

Name-calling should be strictly prohibited.

The following principles will also underscore and reinforce efforts to create a safe classroom environment:

✧ Stress inclusion by discouraging ostracism. Everyone has the right to be part of the group, and all must understand this.

✧ As one might do in a family, develop class rituals, traditions, and legends.

✧ Place high value on positive interpersonal relationships and acknowledge them publicly to the class.

✧ Model the behavior you wish to see among your students. Never forget the enormous impact that your own behavior has in determining class standards.

✧ Never let an opportunity to correct a breach of expectations slip by, however minor it may seem at the time. This may take up more time than you might like at the beginning of the school year, but once the message is made clear through repetition and modeling, the need to use "teachable moments" for this purpose will likely diminish.

The positive benefits of creating a warm, caring environment are many. Kids become more willing to take risks and to participate because they feel safe from external threats to their competence. They feel valued for their efforts and accomplishments, thereby gaining acceptance within the group as a whole. They learn that making an error need not be accompanied by a deafening roar of negative reaction from peers and teachers. Thus, creating a positive environment is the first and most important step in setting the tone at the beginning of a school year. The next step involves direct instruction.

### Provide Direct Instruction: Some Lesson Ideas

Teachers will wonder where they can fit this stuff in. Will it fit under language arts, social studies, guidance, health, or ...? The simple answer is that it doesn't matter. If you can squeak in a forty-five minute session once a week and call it social development or something (in British Columbia it is called personal planning), there will be few parents or administrators who would challenge it. A series of lessons might look like this:

✦ **What is peer pressure?** Using the concepts covered in the first part of this chapter, expose students to the basic concepts of peer pressure—what it is, how it works, how kids cope, and how to resist it.

✦ **Ten responses to overt peer pressure.** Have students write down the following responses to overt peer pressure, being careful to explain when and why each may work:

1. Say no. When pressed for a reason, say "I don't have to give a reason." *(simple refusal)*

2. "I don't want to do that, and I don't have to." *(simple refusal)*

3. "My mother [father] will kill me." *(implies fear of authority)*

4. "I can't. I have to go." *(escapist)*

5. "Nah, let's do something else." *(attempt to divert)*

6. "No thanks, I've tried it and I don't like it." *(states preference)*

7. "If you're going to do that, I'm out of here." *(deflects decision)*

8. "I'm surprised you'd even think about it." *(encourages rethinking)*

9. "No, *not* everybody does it. I don't." *(dispels myth)*

10. "I'd be grounded if my parents found out, and they always find out because my conscience makes me tell them." *(asserts conscience)*

✦ **Offer opportunities for role plays in small groups.** Students internalize the concepts and skills necessary to resist peer pressure if allowed to practice them repeatedly. I like to provide a few scenarios and have groups of three students work together, with one as the Persuader, who attempts to provoke the Resister into complying; one as the Resister, who utilizes an appropriate response; and the third as the Observer, who watches and points out where and when mistakes in strategy may be made.

✦ **Teach students the difference between being assertive and being aggressive.** The role play described above usually deteriorates into an argument when students first try it. This is because the Resister falls into the trap of responding aggressively to aggression from the Persuader. Instead of reaching a resolution, the conflict escalates. At this point, I talk about the differences between being assertive and being aggressive, which will be discussed in more detail in chapter four.

✦ **Teach students the key aspects of assertiveness.** These include eye contact, body language, facial expression, tone and volume of voice, proximity to the aggressor, and choice of words.

✦ **Teach children to de-escalate conflict.** Conflict only escalates when we choose to take the bait. Responding aggressively, seeking revenge, always trying to win, and giving the bully what he wants all serve to escalate conflict until it is beyond the skills of the students to solve without adult intervention. The whole objective is to help kids solve their own conflicts.

✦ **Teach children the difference between acceptable and unacceptable teasing, and insist that they use only acceptable teasing.** Teasing will be discussed further in chapter four, but it is enough to know that what constitutes "only teasing" has broken more hearts and damaged more psyches than can be imagined.

✦ **Use open discussion, role-playing, and debriefing to introduce and reinforce the skills and concepts you wish to see practiced.** Simply hearing or reading something is not enough to internalize it; we have to practice it several times before it becomes part of our everyday behavior.

The content of the "lessons" described above can take months to fully explore. Most of the suggestions for parents that are made later in this chapter can also be adapted and modified for teachers. A teacher is, after all, a dominant adult in the eyes of his students, and as such falls into the same category as parents in the eyes of his students. So strategies that can work for parents can work for teachers too.

### Provide Flexible, Situational Discipline

While the primary objective of any discipline regime is to achieve an acceptable level of individual and group behavior, it is the philosophical base of such a regime that requires our immediate attention. Long lists of restrictive classroom rules with simplified, one-size-fits-all consequences can pose problems. The greatest problem is the creation of rules that are difficult to enforce. To make a rule like "No gum chewing anywhere on the school grounds" compels the rulemaker to ensure that there are sufficient enforcers on the school grounds, clearly an unrealistic expectation. And even if there are sufficient enforcers, the whole basis of effective discipline is lost: the best discipline is self-discipline.

Another problem of blanket consequences is that they ignore the unique circumstances inherent in every act of noncompliance. There are many educators who view fighting as an automatic suspension for both combatants. In my view, the consequences depend entirely on the answers to a number of questions: Are these students chronic offenders or first-timers? Was this a premeditated act on the part of both students, or was it a spontaneous act resulting from a game or misunderstanding? Was one clearly the aggressor, while the other merely tried to defend himself? Are either or both of them genuinely contrite, or do they arrive at the principal's office with chips on their shoulders? The answers to all of these questions demand that each case be judged on its own merits and that the consequences applied should be appropriate to the act, the actors, and the circumstances.

The concept of flexible, situational discipline is difficult for many to accept. They argue that it lacks consistency and that it is unfair. I would argue to the contrary; consistency doesn't mean that we always apply exactly the same consequence for the same transgression; it does mean that we use a consistent approach in dealing with discipline issues.

Flexible, situational discipline is as consistent in its approach as any other regime. As far as being unfair, well, it simply isn't. If the whole point is to make the consequence fit the act, then it would be unfair to do anything but evaluate each case on its own merits. The biggest drawback to a flexible disciplinary regime is that it takes far more "investigative and deliberative time" than a simple "if you do this, then that happens" system. Time is at a premium for teachers, so they often resort to the latter kind of system, the danger being that such a system takes personal responsibility from the child and places it within the framework of an unyielding code of conduct, the consequences of which are applied by the teacher.

## What *Doesn't* Work?

We have seen what *can* work in creating positive relationship skills among students, but what about those things that don't work? The following rarely have any effect:

+ **Drawing lines in the sand.** If you "dare" kids to cross you, or not to comply with your demands, they will cross the line at almost every opportunity. Don't create the conditions that invariably result in power struggles.

+ **Commanding obedience and respect.** Merely commanding these things will not make it so. Kids will obey and respect you not because you are an adult and a teacher, but because you treat them with respect.

+ **Refusal to let them "win" some of the small battles.** Just as parents risk alienating their pre-adolescent children by insisting on complete obedience to every single command, so too will teachers lose if they insist on maintaining an adversarial relationship with their students. Yielding to their wishes in safe, controlled areas will not mean that you are weak or that you are losing; it will mean that you are reasonable and open to changing your mind.

+ **Using verbal shutdowns to suppress dissent or legitimate questions.** This sounds like "Because I said so," "Because I'm the teacher and you're not," "How dare you question me?", "I don't want to hear about it," "That's not my problem," or anything said with sarcasm or cynicism. Even a cursory survey of history tells us that when questioning voices have been suppressed, they have merely gone underground, become stronger, and eventually posed an even greater threat to the status quo.

+ **Ignoring attention-seeking behavior.** Some teachers see such behavior as an attempt to take up more of their time than anyone deserves. In fact, attention-seeking behavior is just that, and the student's need for attention needs to be met somehow, though in a positive and constructive way. If you deny the attention-seeker your attention, you are acting like a doctor who refuses to treat the sick because they are sick.

+ **Using inflexible assignment procedures.** What is more important to you—having the deadline met or seeing that the work actually gets done? Assigning a zero mark to a late assignment does two things: first, it creates animosity in the student, hardly helpful in developing a positive working relationship; and second, it dismisses the late work as meaningless. If punctuality is important, then give a bonus of five marks for all work that is handed in on time, but let that be known to all students at the time the work is assigned. Then, if the student is late, he knows the consequence; thus, he will be consciously choosing to accept the consequence. Personally, I find it ludicrous that a student could actually fail a course for no other reason than that he was chronically late in turning in work.

## In a Nutshell: What Teachers Can Do to Help Kids Deal with Peer Pressure

Creating an atmosphere in which students belong, are accepted, and feel safe is essential to helping students deal with issues stemming from peer pressure. Direct instruction helps students become aware of peer-pressure issues and equips them with skills and strategies to achieve success. Establishing a flexible, situational disciplinary regime encourages students to take responsibility for their own behavior. It will also help them accept responsibility for the choices and decisions they make when influenced by their peers.

More than anything, teachers need to understand how hard it is to be a kid these days. They need to empathize with the problems kids face each day, many far more complex than the ones *they* faced as adolescents. They must adopt a positive view of children, one that sees them not as empty vessels to be filled, but as creative, feeling human beings who need help and guidance to develop the skills of effective adults. Finally, in everything they do, teachers must focus on the main objective: to do as much as possible to facilitate the growth of the whole child. Success in achieving these goals will go a long way to help prepare children for the pressures they will face from their peers in adolescence.

## Ten Ways Parents Can Help Kids Deal with Peer Pressure

First, we must accept the premise that parents are a child's first and most important teachers—that everything a child knows, values, believes, and can do when he first comes to school is a result of home-based learning. This refers not only to the formal teaching of things like tying shoes, printing names, reciting numbers to a hundred, and so on, but also to a child's way of viewing the world, relating to other people, assuming responsibility, and to his values, attitudes, and beliefs. Few of these are taught directly, but rather are absorbed through the child's watching, listening, emulating, and being reinforced for successfully displaying those attributes that his parents value.

Children, both consciously and unconsciously, mimic the behavior they see modeled, especially that modeled by their parents. All parents have experienced those moments when we see glimpses of our personalities expressed by our kids, and we're not always thrilled with what we see. That's why, as parents, we have to have a vision of the kind of children we want to raise, and then seek out and use strategies and techniques that will help them become capable adolescents and adults.

So what can parents do? Here are ten ideas.

1. **Understand your adolescent's need to fit in.** If this means he absolutely must have certain clothing or footwear, don't fight it, as long as the family budget can absorb the shock.

2. **Resist the urge to tighten the bonds.** As kids enter adolescence, they want the freedom to make more choices about the things that affect them the most directly. What a parent could reasonably expect when the child was eight or nine can no longer be expected as a matter of course. They want to fly a bit, but can't if you clip their wings.

3. **Keep your kids busy.** This doesn't mean that they have to be going to five different classes, practices, or games every week. They still need time just to be kids and to do kid things. The old maxim that busy hands are happy hands is bunk. The real needs you are trying to meet are the kids' needs for belonging and acceptance. And if your children show any kind of talent *and express a genuine interest* in something, create the conditions that allow them to participate. Then stand back and support them all the way.

4. **Don't buy them clothes that you like.** Adolescents are incredibly conscious about their personal appearance, and your tastes will almost certainly differ. Never mind that the pink sweater would look really good on your daughter, and pink has always been her favorite color. If the texture and shape are not right, if the label isn't prestigious enough, and if the color of the month happens to be black, forget it. You'll avoid countless arguments.

5. **Avoid a constant battle of wills.** Know your minimum acceptable outcome, then negotiate from there. You also need to know when to back down and give in, because kids have to win once in a while too, just to let them know that you can be reasonable and that issues are worthy of discussion. This approach should only relate to relatively safe issues, not the biggies. The kid who is always told *no* stops asking after a while and can become adept at hiding what is really going on in his life.

6. **Acknowledge the influence of peers.** Talk about it coolly and rationally, and empathize with your kids about how hard it is to be an individual. If kids get a sense that you really *do* understand what it is like for them, they may well feel more open about talking to you about their fears and concerns. The most common frustration expressed by parents of adolescents is that the kids just won't talk to them anymore. Keeping the lines of communication open helps, both by talking to the kids and by listening to what they say.

7. **Don't forbid your kids to associate with certain so-called friends.** By doing this, you are taking the decision away from the adolescent. Your objective is to ensure that your child not succumb to negative influences, but issuing orders, threats, or ultimatums doesn't work. Kids don't set out to defy you just because you are their parents, but they do want the freedom to make their own decisions. If you have done everything else possible to keep communication open, to foster healthy self-esteem, to demonstrate your trust in their ability to make sound judgments, they will usually make the right choices.

8. **Start to build your kids' self-esteem, confidence, judgment, and the ability to make choices and decisions when they are very young.** None of these qualities and capabilities can emerge from a void. As adults, we must be keenly aware of the importance of using the best possible means to provide our children with the best chance for success.

9. **If you must apply consequences, make sure your children know why it is necessary.** Don't tell them that they are grounded for two weeks because they have disappointed [or angered or frustrated] you. Tell them that they disobeyed, or that they willfully made a bad choice or decision, or that their action caused someone pain or injury. Make it clear that since they knew the consequences for their actions beforehand, they *chose* to take the action they did. Avoid saying something that suggests that they let *you* down; the message implicit in that kind of statement is that their role is to please *you*, not to please themselves.

10. **Let your children use you as a scapegoat.** If your kids feel cornered, they can always tell their friends that their parents will find out and that they don't want to risk invoking the wrath of Mom or Dad. In this way, they may manage to avoid problematic situations and still save face. Saving face is incredibly important for kids subject to peer pressure.

## More Powerful Than a Locomotive

Peer pressure is the often unspoken pressure felt by an adolescent to fit in. *Not* fitting in results in all kinds of unpleasant circumstances, up to and including suicide. Parents can help lessen the effects of peer pressure by developing kids' strength of character, decision-making ability, sense of morals and ethics, self-esteem, and a sense of belonging and acceptance by providing a safe environment. Teachers and principals can help by augmenting the work of parents, by working closely with them, and by viewing the child from a positive perspective.

Peer pressure is indeed more powerful than a locomotive, but children can be prepared to deal with it through the concerted efforts of parents and teachers. This is not to say that they won't rebel anyway; but if they do, it will be because they have been able to properly assess the consequences of noncompliance and are prepared to take their lumps. And as adults who are trying to raise independent children who can think for themselves and make their own decisions, we must accept that they will. Only at that point will we be able to look at our efforts with some satisfaction and be able to say "We did what we had to do," and leave it at that.

# 4.

# Bullying, Put-downs, and Teasing: Thorns in Our Flesh

## About Eddy

*Every neighborhood has at least one bully and, as a kid, mine was no exception. Eddy Black was probably the Wayne Gretzky of bullydom, and most of the kids in the neighborhood and at school lived with the fearful near-certainty that sooner or later Eddy would turn on them.*

*Eddy was the first person I'd ever met who consistently looked for the wrong thing to do. If we were walking down a back alley, it was Eddy who would tip over garbage cans and run like the devil. If a bunch of us tried a surreptitious raid on a cherry tree, it was Eddy who would throw the fruit at the windows of the people who owned the tree. If someone got a better mark on a test and made the mistake of telling him, Eddy would rough him up. If someone beat him fair and square in a race or athletic competition, Eddy would pick a fight and end up pounding the kid. To Eddy, everything was a competition and he simply had to be first or best or fastest or boldest.*

*Needless to say, he'd cheat, trip, punch, or find any other way he could to sabotage and humiliate others, even if it was something as simple as Monopoly or math bingo. He had two kinds of friends: those he had bullied and who wanted to avoid future beatings, and those who tended to be bullies themselves. In some unspoken way they seemed to divide up their turf, in much the same way as criminal syndicates might divide up a city or town. The only thing that was certain was that not a day* went by that Eddy wasn't in some sort of conflict, whether with classmates or adult authority figures like teachers, parents, or the police.

Eddy was a master at using verbal put-downs to maximum destructive effect. The term WEAKLING was one of his favorites; when he called someone WEAKLING it implied that he was stronger. If the target of his taunts took the bait, he would proceed to demonstrate his superior combative abilities. He also used teasing to provoke responses, and his teasing was always a cruel exploitation of something over which the target had no real control. Eddy was like a persistent itch that wouldn't go away—always there, always irritating, and always a threat to peaceful existence.

In later grades, as we all began to become aware of the world beyond our own yards and streets, Eddy was less promi-nent as a bully, though not because he'd come to any flash of insight about changing his behavior. As we moved on to a two-thousand-student high school, Eddy became only one of dozens of minor-league bullies fighting for top spot in the pecking order. Eddy had finally run up against the bane of all bullies: bigger, tougher, meaner bullies. Silent cheers went up from dozens of Eddy's former victims when he was finally disempowered by some of these toughs. By grade nine, he'd faded into a sort of lonely anonymity, and I can honestly say I don't know what ever became of him.

Looking back, and having worked with scores of Eddys in my years as an educator, I think I can now account for the reason why Eddy was the way he was. He was the only child of parents who fought and argued virtually full time, often fueled by alcohol. They seemed to believe that they could make Eddy behave by yelling at him and belting him when they were displeased, which was frequently. They used put-downs and sarcasm like a drunkard uses alcohol, frequently and without thought.

Eddy was essentially powerless at home, and I can never remember him going anywhere or doing anything with his mother and father. They didn't go on holidays together, and he spent most of his summers wandering around looking for excitement. Call it "attention-seeking behavior." In retrospect,

*Eddy was probably a very unhappy boy who tried to gain personal power by lording it over others in much the same way as his parents lorded it over him.*

Despite the views of a few highly controversial behaviorists, it is pretty safe to assume that nobody is born a bully. Bullying is a behavioral pattern that appears to have its roots in whatever has caused these kids to become powerless in their personal lives. There is both good news and bad news in this: the good news is that behavior *can* be modified; the bad news is that such change requires massive effort, patience, and the willingness to concede that the attempt may fail.

Bullying is about using whatever tools are available to gain power and control, to elevate the bully's feelings of self-esteem, and to achieve status within the peer group. Bullies use provocative language and physical violence to create and enhance their sense of control over others. Lacking positive experiences, they opt to earn success in negative ways that elicit attention from teachers and parents (other adults too) and that instill fear in most of their peers. Bullying, in essence, is a deliberate attempt to manipulate others for the bully's own personal satisfaction.

Put-downs are one tool the bully uses, but the act of putting others down is committed by many others, often without the bully's goal of control. These put-downs are a less calculated and more spontaneous response to others, at least in a defensive sense. Put-downs used as an offensive tactic are closer to bullying and achieve similar results: a measure of power and control. Again, put-downs are more difficult to stop because they become a pattern of behavior for a far greater number than does bullying.

Teasing is also employed by the bully and the put-down artist, but the major difference is that teasing is sometimes acceptable. I can call my good friend a jerk, and he takes no offense because we both know I don't mean it. Our friendship is based on a wide range of shared experience, beliefs, values, and aspirations, so when he calls me a dweeb, I don't get angry. Still, teasing can be just as great a source of pain and anguish as bullying if it is unwelcome. The key understanding the teaser must possess is to know what is acceptable, and when.

Bullying, put-downs, and teasing are major issues for a whole lot of reasons, not the least of which is that each causes anxiety among classmates and kids in the neighborhood. Such anxiety in the classroom detracts from students' ability to absorb what is being taught and practiced. Scared and threatened children don't learn very well, and educators who choose to ignore the social and emotional climate as they blithely waltz through the curriculum are not serving their students as well as they could. At the risk of sounding overly repetitive, the classroom has to be a supportive, safe, and enabling environment. Bullying, put-downs, and unwelcome teasing are impediments to achieving such an environment.

While not every bully fits the same profile as Eddy, there are similarities and tendencies among most of them. We must have an understanding of the complex issues associated with bullying, put-downs, and teasing so that we can become better equipped to help both the bully and the bullied.

## Bullying: The First Thorn

We will probably encounter bullies throughout our lives, from the kid who scribbles all over our kindergarten masterpieces, to the kid on the soccer field who trips us if we try to get by him, to power-drunk adults who simply want to wield their power, to the boss who makes life difficult for us just because he can do so without fear of reprisal. Our natural instincts are twofold: to protect ourselves and to get back at the bully. We use a number of strategies to accomplish both, but the most important concept in dealing with bullies, and one that is sort of a rallying cry, is this: *If you give a bully what he wants, the bully wins.*

So, what is bullying, and what are its underlying bases? The ideas that follow are helpful in thinking about this question.

✦ **Bullying is another way of gaining and wielding power.** Power is the absolute number one issue with bullies, and every issue, no matter how insignificant to others, is a power issue. Bullies can't bear to lose, and losing face or sense of dignity will always invite an attempt to regain power. Bullies find they like the feeling of power and tend to want more, thus beginning a cycle of bullying with no foreseeable end.

✦ **Bullying is a means of gaining self-esteem by diminishing the self-esteem of others.** In effect, the bully can't bear the success of others, seeing such success not as success for the other person, but as failure for himself. In chapter 2, we saw that success, and reinforcement of that success, plays an integral part in our feelings of self-esteem. The bully, who usually lacks self-esteem due to limited experience with success and reinforcement, simply seeks to feel better by making others feel worse. In a twisted sort of way, he experiences success and an elevation of self-esteem through completely negative means. In essence, he steals it from someone who has a higher level of self-esteem than he does.

✦ **Bullying is an attempt to carve out and extend a sphere of control.** Power is the key issue, but maintaining control of a group of living, changing people requires continual bullying activity. Very frequently, bullies come from a controlling home environment where there is no room for discussion or negotiation, where they are directed to shut up and do what they are told, or where every decision is made for them and they darned well better like it. Put simply, the only thing they can even try to control is the world outside the home and family.

✦ **Bullying is an attempt to gain peer status.** In some ways, every bully thinks that if he can't have status as a good student, a good athlete, or a well-liked person, then he'll seek a reputation as the toughest, strongest, meanest kid in the school. In a somewhat skewed feat of logic, he believes that such a position will bring him respect. More likely, he will be feared and disdained, but quietly so as not to invite attack.

✦ **Bullying sometimes emerges from a distorted view of what is truly funny.** "Funny" to these kids normally involves pain, suffering, or humiliation. Bullies are the ones who think it is uproariously funny if someone falls and is injured. They find continual amusement in the classroom mistakes of others and are quick to point out the weaknesses they perceive in others. Sadly, some of our popular television shows tend to reinforce this type of humor. Watch "America's Funniest Home Videos" or "America's Funniest People" and make note of how many of the clips shown involve someone getting hurt or humiliated. Bullies love these shows.

✦ **Bullying sometimes emerges from serious personality disorders beyond the scope of all but professional psychologists/psychiatrists.** In psychology, there is a personality type called a sociopath. These very rare individuals are absolutely uncaring of others and appear to have no conscience at all. Sociopaths can cause great pain and suffering without any emotion or any kind of remorse. While they are rare, they do exist, and if one of your students appears to fit these characteristics, get help for him.

There are other aspects to the concept of bullying that deserve attention. In a fight-freeze-flee situation, bullies will always choose to fight; freezing and fleeing are simply not options. Neither is a win-win scenario even a possibility; bullies want nothing more than total victory. As far as conflict goes, these kids see escalation as the goal of conflict, not as an impediment to resolving it. In fact, escalation is a bullying strategy used to provoke a response that gives the bully tacit permission to administer his own brand of punishment.

In some ways, too, bullying is about setting up expectations for future behavior. As victims or observers of victims, classmates and peers learn that the bully can hurt them at any time in the future for little or no apparent reason. This obviously fuels the bully's feelings of power and control, as well as his sense of self-esteem. He will employ elaborate verbal and physical strategies to maintain his control.

## What Does Bullying Look Like?

Bullies do a variety of things in their attempt to gain attention, to strike fear into the hearts of others, or simply to "flex their bullying muscles" for all to see. Most of these actions fall under the following categories:

+ **Acts intended to cause pain:** spitting, punching, kicking, slapping, pinching, biting, scratching, striking, tripping, choking, and, more serious, cutting, stabbing, strangling, shooting

+ **Acts of petty vandalism:** breaking, hiding, discarding, stealing, destroying, confiscating, or vandalizing the personal belongings of others

+ **Acts that "level the playing field" in sports:** playing dirty, cheating to win, and beating up any challengers

## What Does Bullying Sound Like?

Bullies use provocative language to coax their targets into responding. They believe that they have carte blanche to say whatever they want and, if the target rises to the challenge, the bully will unleash the weapons in his considerable arsenal. These statements are only samples:

"Wanna make something out of it?"
"I could beat you up with one hand tied behind my back."
"Go ahead, take the first punch."
"Take that back or I'll pound you."
"You're dead after school."
"If I see you out of your yard, I'll get you."
"You're too stupid to live."
"You suck."
"Everyone knows you're a slut [gay]."
"You think you're smarter than me?"
"You'll do what I tell you to do."
"I'm the toughest kid in the school."
"You had it coming."
"What's the matter, can't you take it?"
"I'm going to teach you a lesson."

## The Attributes of Bullies

Bullies use name-calling, shouting, and sarcasm to elicit the kind of response they want to hear. But these overt actions really only scratch the surface in describing bullies. There are many more attributes shared by most bullies.

+ **Bullies lack impulse control.** These are the kids who "shoot first and ask questions later." The rational consideration of alternatives is as foreign to them as a blizzard is to a camel.

+ **Bullies lack anger-management skills.** Being angry is normal and natural, but bullies tend to play out the same, tired anger scenarios over and over again. This is intensely frustrating to anyone having to deal with the results.

+ **Bullies often can't see the connection between actions and consequences.** They tend to believe that they are in trouble only because they got caught, or because an adult is mean.

+ **Bullies display a penchant for blaming the victim.** This relates to the unwillingness of people with low self-esteem— in this case bullies—to accept that they have made an error. Mistakes are equated with being bad, wrong, stupid, or otherwise unacceptable.

+ **Bullies often display a persecution complex.** Because they are often in trouble with adult authorities, and because they just as often fail to see the relationship between their own negative actions and the logical but unpleasant consequences of those actions, they see the trouble as nothing more than someone picking on them.

+ **Bullies appear "mad at the world."** Unwilling or unable to express their resentments to parents or teachers, bullies pack around a great deal of unresolved conflict that spills out and is directed at their peers.

+ **Bullies are intensely competitive, even in areas they can't possibly win.** These kids can't stand to lose, since losing leads to the negative feedback they wish to avoid. They will use any means at their disposal to win.

+ **Bullies are socially inept.** For all the obvious reasons, most related to trust, few people want to be bosom buddies with bullies. And as bullies' relations with others are all based on conflict, they have no idea how to form and maintain lasting friendships.

+ **Bullies have poor decision-making skills.** If competent decision making requires a calm, rational consideration of alternatives, then the bully is sabotaged by his own inability to be anything other than aggressively reactive in any conflict.

+ **Bullies have an abnormally high tolerance for conflict.** Practice makes perfect, goes the old adage, and with bullies it is especially accurate. Some actually appear to revel in conflict, never sure what to do or how to behave when conflict is absent.

+ **Bullies lack empathy.** These kids are very egocentric and are rarely able to relate to or even understand the pain and anguish they cause others. On the contrary, their measure of success is that they are *able* to cause pain and anguish.

+ **Bullies believe revenge is an obligation, not a choice.** They constantly seek to even the score over real or imagined slights or insults. Note that it is the bully who decides what affronts his sensibilities, and his view of reality can be distorted by all kinds of flawed logic. Thus, you never know what to expect from a bully—or when.

It is clear that bullies and bullying are more than simple schoolyard problems that can be fixed or cured with the application of disciplinary consequences like detentions or suspensions. Bullies have complex personalities that took years to develop, and the meting out of routine punishments will no more fix the problem than would applying a cold compress to the forehead of someone suffering a brain tumor.

We are compelled to look at the totality of the child's life to try to figure out why bullies are the way they are. As in Eddy Black's situation, poor parenting is frequently a major factor. If we recall the discussion of mind-set, modeling, and method from chapter two, some light might be shed on the emergence of bullies in our neighborhoods and schools. While not all bullies will come from the environment de-scribed below, it is reasonably safe to say that the factors discussed frequently lead to bullying.

## Mind-set That Contributes to Bullying

The parental mind-set that leads to children becoming bullies includes a number of beliefs that can generally be characterized as provocative. Kids are taught that might is right, that if you are threatened you must fight back—and fight to win. They are also taught that winning is everything, that failing means they are failures as people, and that we, here in this house, are okay; it's the rest of the world that's messed up.

These parents have a simplistic view of what it is to raise children. They believe that telling them something often enough will make it so, that their word is gospel, and that children are very definitely of lesser status than adults. In some ways they treat their children like empty-headed little things whose heads must be filled with the "right ways to behave." At the same time, these children must never challenge or question parental authority.

Further, these parents tend to believe in relatively severe physical punishment, believing that inflicting pain will reduce the possibility that similar actions will be repeated. Kids with these kinds of parents learn that bigger and stronger is always right; that if someone doesn't agree with you, you should view them as a threat; and that threats should be met with quick, decisive, and violent action.

All in all, these parents tend to look at others from a deficiency point of view. They are generally suspicious of others and therefore seek to find the bad, the inept, or the weak. Cynicism and sarcasm are common, and disparaging the accomplishments of others is a daily exercise. It is little wonder that children from homes like these have trouble getting along with others.

## Modeling That Contributes to Bullying

Of course there are adult bullies too. In fact, it is not at all unusual for those who are bullies as children to refine and polish their bullying skills well into adulthood. It is reasonable to assume, then, that adult bullies model these skills for their own children, often bullying their own kids. The modeling that contributes to bullying is the physical expression of the mind-set that accompanies it.

In homes that help create bullies, conflict is a daily occurrence. Yelling and arguing are commonplace, and physical means are sometimes resorted to in order to make a point or to win an argument. Provocative language is used, with threats and demeaning comments tossed freely about. Doors get slammed, dishes get thrown, and lines get drawn in the sand, with other people being dared to cross them. What nobody does is sit down and talk about things in a calm, rational, or understanding way.

None of this is to suggest that all bullies come from this type of environment, but the chances of a bully emerging from this type of home are high. Some readers may know bullies that come from very different homes, homes they might characterize as good ones, where yelling and screaming are absent, where kids are never spanked or hit, and where the parents are caring, open people. In these cases, there must be other reasons for bullying. Perhaps the children are simply the subjects of too much parental control and concern. Perhaps these are the kids who have no voice in what they do, where they go, what they wear, or what they are permitted to question. Maybe they've never been allowed to make important decisions and they feel powerless at home. Perhaps they are children whose behavior has never been subject to corrective action by their parents, so they think they can do whatever they want. Most kids—most people for that matter—will push as far as they can before the limits are set out for them. If there are no limits set, then there is no concept of how far is "too far." In other words, bullies are sometimes those who have never had to be accountable, so think they can do anything they want to gain the power they feel they lack at home or in the classroom.

## Coping Methods Used by the Bullied

To this point, we have explored a wide variety of concepts that attempt to explain bullies and their motivations. Essentially obsessed with power and control, and getting as much of it as they can, bullies are obviously a problem to those kids who want nothing more than to be left alone without taunts and torments thrown their way. This group is the cannon fodder of the bully. The bullied adopt the following coping mechanisms out of sheer self-interest rooted in the desire for self-preservation:

- **Comply with the bully.** These kids either say nothing or readily comply with the demands of the bully. They are passive and cave in, lick their wounds, and move on in the fervent hope that the bully will lose interest in taunting them. They are often the easiest targets for the bully because he knows he can always exert power and control over them without fear of resistance.

- **Ally with the bully.** A bully will enlist the aid and support of those who fear him, reasoning that strength in numbers lends him credibility and control. Those who ally themselves with a bully understand that this does not preclude the bully turning on them from time to time, but in balancing resistance with support, they are betting that they'll usually be able to avoid his wrath.

- **Avoid the bully.** In a manner similar to those wanting to avoid unpleasant peer pressure, these kids adopt the blue grouse strategy. If you remember, this strategy consists of standing absolutely still, hoping not to be noticed. Although often successful in the short run, it is almost inevitable that they will eventually be noticed and become the object of the bully's tactics.

- **Seek assistance from more powerful adults.** This coping mechanism is rarely used because of the very real fear that the bully will find out who squealed and will eventually retaliate with equal or excessive force. It is used only with the assurance of complete anonymity.

- **Meet fire with fire.** Also very rare, this requires that the bullied literally fight back. This approach is markedly different from one that employs assertiveness, which will be discussed later.

- **Escape from the bully.** This strategy includes everything from simply walking or running away to adopting elaborate strategies to stay home from school. This is a dead-end approach because seeking refuge in the safety of the home is only a temporary measure; everyone eventually has to venture out into the world and cope with individuals who can make our lives miserable.

✦ **Be assertive in resisting the bully.** Another rare approach, usually because of little or no awareness of the fundamental differences between aggressiveness and assertiveness. A bully has a difficult time egging an assertive person into a fight, because assertiveness is a way of holding firm without provoking retaliation.

## Assertiveness: The Most Effective Strategy for Dealing with Bullies

Assertiveness is an often misunderstood concept, with many believing that it means to stand our ground, trade provocative comment for provocative comment, and win the conflict through superior verbal abilities. This more accurately describes aggressiveness and results in escalation of conflict, not in de-escalation. Being assertive actually involves stating your position firmly but clearly without throwing fuel on the fire of conflict. Not an easy task, but with training and practice, a manageable one. Assertiveness says "This is my position," while aggressiveness says "This is my position, you stupid idiot."

There are six major aspects to assertiveness.

1. **Eye contact.** It is a natural reaction to want to avoid eye contact with someone who is verbally attacking, ridiculing, or taunting us. The bully knows this, so when we face up to him and maintain steady eye contact, he can find it unnerving. It is important, though, not to glare, but to look at him as though you were watching a parade go by—engaged but neutral.

2. **Facial expression.** When we are under attack, a worried or even angry facial expression, which mirrors our inner anxiety, is quite normal. An expression of fear, or one of defiance, can subtly escalate the conflict in the mind of the bully, who is a master at taking cues from any evidence of resistance or anger. This is why it is useful to adopt a neutral facial expression.

3. **Body language.** Instinctively, we tend to turn away, quite literally, from unpleasantness, and this is certainly true when we are being provoked by a bully. It is important to face the bully squarely. I suggest to kids that they

should form an imaginary triangle with their shoulders at an equal distance from the bully's chin. The bully may try to cause the bullied to back off, but the assertive opponent will stand his ground without provoking the bully. Clenched fists can also be interpreted by the bully as a threat, so it is important that hands be kept unclenched.

4. **Proximity.** While it is difficult to know if and when to back down, it is equally important not to place yourself too close to the bully. He may feel that you are encroaching on his personal space in a threatening way. Keep your distance, but don't back up unless it is obvious you are about to be physically attacked.

5. **Tone of voice.** Critically important, tone of voice is very difficult to control, since the anger that results from provocation is difficult to manage. A clear, steady tone is the goal. Whining, sarcasm, yelling, or any attempt to one-up the bully will be interpreted as a willingness to escalate the conflict, which is exactly what the bully wants.

6. **Choice of words.** While specific verbal patterns and strategies are discussed in "Responses to Bullying, Put-downs, and Unwelcome Teasing" on pages 118-124, it is enough to know that the choice of words often determines whether or not the conflict will escalate or be defused. Name-calling, trading insults, and other forms of verbal provocation are by far the most common precipitators of fights and arguments. It is tempting to fight back with words, but doing so is just as provocative as throwing a punch.

Aggressiveness is markedly different from assertiveness, and is a very negative response to bullying. Eye contact is generally steady and threatening, as is facial expression. Threatening body language includes clenched fists, feigned or actual punching, bumping, or shoving. Those who are aggressive, including bullies, often use encroachment on a victim's personal space as a means of exerting power and control. Their tone of voice is antagonistic, threatening, insulting, sarcastic, and/or demeaning, all aimed at provoking a negative response. The words they choose usually include profanities, insults, unwelcome teasing, cruel comments about some physical or intellectual attribute, or promises to inflict pain and suffering—all very unpleasant for the person under attack.

The task for the bullied is to somehow get past the urge to fight back, and be assertive. Similarly, the ability to outthink the bully while behaving assertively is key to successful self-protection. The bullied need to practice resisting the urge to fight, freeze, or flee and instead should stand their ground without inviting a violent response. Though admittedly difficult, such an approach is possible through direct instruction and frequent opportunities to practice the skills. Before turning to the skills, however, a closer look at put-downs and teasing is useful to gain a broader perspective on the whole concept of bullying.

## In a Nutshell: Bullying

When little attention is paid to the pain and suffering of the bullied, all kinds of negative spinoffs result. They become frightened, living in constant fear of being physically or emotionally battered, and can become socially withdrawn. Such withdrawal can feed the fires of depression and profound sadness and, if the bullied person already happens to be a social outcast, can create an emotional environment where suicide becomes a viable alternative. Recent reports out of Japan document acts of suicide by high school students no longer able to cope with schoolyard bullies. Readers will recall the story of Alan in the preceding chapter; continuous, overwhelming bullying from a wide variety of schoolmates was undoubtedly a major factor in his decision to hang himself.

Regardless of the motivations of the bully and the impact he has on the bullied, it is clear that creating an environment in which bullying is minimized or eliminated requires a two-pronged approach. Prong number one is to work with the bully, trying to understand his motivations and attempting to help him change or otherwise modify his bullying characteristics and habits. This requires an understanding of the roots and patterns of bullying and a clear commitment to patience, a modicum of tolerance, and a willingness to believe that behavioral change is possible.

Prong number two, and one we often neglect because of the time and energy required to deal with the actions of the bully, is to help the bullied learn and practice skills and concepts that help them cope with bullies. All the old ideas, like "just ignore it" or "fight back," will do nothing more than provide additional bullying opportunities as well as increase the possibility that conflict will be escalated. It is impossible to ignore bullies because they are masters at provocation, and it is difficult to fight back because, again, bullies are often better fighters than almost everyone.

In simple terms, the goals are to decrease the bullies' incidents of bullying while simultaneously helping the other kids resist without provoking a violent response. A useful way to do the latter is to introduce, explore, and practice the skills of assertiveness.

## Put-downs: Another Thorn in Our Flesh

While bullies are masters of putting other people down, the verbal put-down is far more widespread among kids and less deliberate than the actions of the bully. If the bully acts to elicit a response, the typical kid uses put-downs for different reasons. One is to respond to a put-down directed at him by another kid—a kind of vengeful act that seeks to one-up the other person. A second is to gain status as a quick-witted comedian who others approve and enjoy for his creative comments. A third is simply to get a rise out of the other person to start a battle of words or wits. Put-downs, though, can be just as hurtful to the recipient as direct, physical bullying.

Put-downs are not limited to verbal barbs and jabs. Other ways of putting someone down include spreading false rumors or heaping unfounded criticism on someone. Still another method is the exaggerated mimicking of someone's characteristics—voice, way of talking or walking, facial expressions, and so on—with the intent of causing others to laugh. Even things as simple as getting up and moving away or holding one's nose when a kid sits close by can legitimately be considered put-downs. The worst, however, is the verbal put-down, since it is clearly and unmistakably aimed directly at one person.

We've all heard the ancient adage "Sticks and stones may break my bones, but names will never hurt me." Whoever came up with that little gem wasn't thinking too clearly. The reality is that "sticks and stones may break my bones, but words can scar my soul." A black eye, a cut lip, a bleeding nose will all heal relatively quickly, but being called a faggot, a slut, or a nerd repeatedly over a long time causes deep emotional wounds that fester for what seems like forever. If most bullying results in physical pain or discomfort, then put-downs work on the mind, the self-perception, and the self-esteem of the person being put-down.

Most adults have observed that kids are particularly adept at finding vulnerability and exploiting it. This is the essence of put-downs. In some ways, the same motivations that cause a bully to become a bully are employed by those who use put-downs. Put-downs, while not necessarily intending to demean, devalue, embarrass, or hurt, nevertheless do just that. For the most part, put-downs are a prime example of a win-lose ethic, and the kids who are adept at using them enjoy winning these verbal showdowns. Often, these kids do not realize that what they are doing causes real, tangible pain; to them it's just a game, just teasing, or just having fun. They do not yet understand that having fun at the expense of others is a pretty negative way to derive enjoyment from life.

## Which Kids Are Most Susceptible to Put-downs?

Some types of kids seem to be more susceptible to put-downs than others. Some of these include:

✦ **Kids with weaker, fragile egos.** Kids who are demonstrably less confident or shy are less likely to fight or argue back, so they become easy targets for put-downs. Sounds like: "What's the matter, baby, forget to change your diaper?"

+ **High achievers who tend toward egomania.** Nobody likes to be shown up, so kids who constantly boast of their successes quickly become tedious, and therefore targets for put-downs. Sounds like: "So what if you got straight A's, everyone thinks you're a dweeb anyway."

+ **Kids who are physically "different."** It is easy to find characteristics of others to pick on, particularly things they have no immediate control over, things like wearing glasses; being too tall, too short, too fat, or too skinny; having oddly shaped or unusual features, bad skin, a high voice, or crooked teeth; having an unusual personality—and so on into infinity. Put-downs aimed at characteristics like these are especially hurtful because they are directed at the easily observable and indefensible. Sounds like: "Chubby." "Four-eyes." "Pizza face." "Moron." And countless others.

+ **Loners.** These are the kids who choose to be alone, for whatever reasons. Their social skills are poor or absent and they often have different interests than the other kids. Often, too, they are quite bright, resulting in their being termed nerds, a term usually used to denote a bright person with no social skills. Sounds like: "Space cadet." "Nerd." "Geek."

Reactions from kids who are subjected to repeated put-downs are identical to those of the bullied: withdrawal, depression, sadness, anger, acting out, and/or destructiveness. Sometimes, too, silent revenge is the reaction, with damage done anonymously to the put-down artist's belongings. Kids who are constantly put down can also become ostracized and have great trouble relating to and with others. Self-esteem takes a beating, making these kids all the more vulnerable to negative peer pressure as they move to high school. There are few students who can rise above put-downs, since they are always very personal.

The role of the classroom teacher with respect to put-downs is twofold. First, the teacher should ensure that none of his own comments to students could possibly be construed as put-downs. This is the "modeling" approach, recognizing that students will tend to assume those characteristics they see and hear in the classroom and that appear to be acceptable to the teacher. Second, it must be made clear to all students that put-downs are not acceptable. A discussion of what constitutes a put-down, why put-downs are unacceptable, what effect they have on the recipient, and appropriate ways of expressing feelings should be conducted. This relates directly to discussions earlier in this book about creating a safe physical, emotional, and psychological environment in the classroom.

## In a Nutshell: Put-downs

Although it is reasonable to assert that all bullies use put-downs, it does not follow that all who use put-downs are bullies. Put-downs are often used to defend against verbal attacks from others, so often have a defensive flavor. Still, some of the motivations for put-downs are strikingly similar to those of bullies.

Put-downs can sometimes be considered preemptive, where the acquisition or consolidation of personal power and/or peer group status is the goal. The idea here is to instill fear or respect in others so that they'll think twice before initiating conflict. At other times put-downs are reactive, a defense against real or perceived threats. Kids who are reactive are sometimes quite thin-skinned and hypersensitive to the words, actions, and even the accomplishments of others. They consider any judgmental comment, intended or not, as the first shot in the war of words. Because they have a shaky sense of personal power, they will not accept anything from anybody who threatens to erode their own power further.

In some ways, put-downs are a more serious problem than bullying, simply because there are considerably fewer kids who qualify as bullies than the number of kids who daily employ put-downs. Both carry the potential for initiating physical violence, which is a whole other issue, but which is similarly about power and control. One thing seems certain: if kids are permitted to put each other down, consistently and regularly, any other attempt at conflict resolution training is pointless. The task, then, is to employ strategies that will defuse and de-escalate put-downs. Such strategies are outlined on pages 118-124.

# Teasing: Yet Another Thorn

If I had a dollar for every time a kid sent to me for disciplinary reasons said, "But I was just teasing ...," I'd have been able to retire comfortably years ago. The words "just teasing" are used to convey the idea that teasing is not at all negative, and just why anyone would get mad because he was being teased is certainly a mystery. Teasing is really just another form of put-down and, in some ways, another way of bullying. Many kids become genuinely confused when the people they've teased lose it completely. They just don't get it.

For purposes of definition, let's consider teasing an attempt to have fun or create humor about someone else's characteristics, actions, habits, or other attributes. These include physical characteristics such as height, weight, stature, hair, teeth, eyes, clothing, and footwear. It can also include other attributes such as intelligence, academic ability, athletic prowess, beliefs, attitudes, values, aspirations, and likes and dislikes. Anyone who differs from his peer group in any way is a candidate for teasing. Not all teasing, however, is totally unwelcome.

## Acceptable vs. Unacceptable Teasing

Teasing falls into two categories: acceptable and unacceptable. Acceptable teasing has the following characteristics:

+ **It is done by a trusted, close friend or family member.** If someone we are close to makes a teasing comment, we can usually accept it because we know it is not meant to provoke or anger us.

+ **It is not repeated continually to exhaust our patience and make us angry.** When bullies and put-down artists try our patience, they call it *teasing;* however, the victim calls it *bullying.*

+ **It isn't meant to hurt.** If, by chance, it does hurt, the teaser usually observes this and makes amends either by apologizing or, at the least, stopping the teasing.

+ **It is not directed at something over which we have no control.** Unusual or atypical physical characteristics normally provide enough personal anxiety in themselves; being teased about them only makes things worse.

+ **It is said to the person, not about the person.** Being teased in front of a group is never particularly comfortable.

+ **The tone is friendly and devoid of sarcasm or cynicism.** We can sometimes accept teasing if we see there is no malice intended.

Unacceptable teasing displays directly the opposite characteristics of those listed above. In short, unacceptable teasing occurs when it originates from someone other than a friend or relative and when it is intended to hurt. The teaser does this by picking on something over which the teased has no immediate control and repeating it—sometimes mercilessly—in front of a larger group. The tone is derisive or hurtful and is more often said *about* the person than to him. While teasing is similar to put-downs and bullying, the main difference is that teasing is sometimes acceptable or welcome, whereas put-downs and bullying are *never* acceptable or welcome.

The reactions or responses to unwelcome teasing are not much different from the reactions to put-downs and bullying. Emotional pain, anger, frustration, sadness, depression, withdrawal, violence, and revenge, either overt or covert, are common. The problem that most kids have when they tease others is that they don't understand that the target of the teasing may not feel that it is either welcome or acceptable, even when the teaser intends no malice. This is the crux of the teasing issue: the teaser and the teased have different ideas about what is acceptable, and the degree to which they differ on this can be the stimulus for a major conflict that catches the teaser completely off guard. It is therefore imperative for teachers and parents to ensure that kids understand the difference between welcome and unwelcome teasing and that unwelcome teasing has the potential for sudden and violent retaliation.

# What Can Teachers Do to Help?

Dealing with the problems of bullying, put-downs, and teasing requires the two-pronged approach mentioned earlier. The first prong is to work with the bully, put-down artist, or teaser in the areas of anger management, impulse control, empathy, tolerance, and decision making. Reinforcing the concepts of personal responsibility may also help, along with trying to provide opportunities for him to experience positive success and the reinforcement that accompanies it. In other words, work on the underlying causes of the behavior and avoid the temptation to simply apply sanctions to the behavioral expression of the causes. Admittedly, not a simple task, but surely one that should have a more long-lasting effect than a detention or suspension.

The second prong is to help the entire class learn how to avoid being bullied, put down, or teased. If other students can respond without escalating the conflict, pretty soon the bully will have no one to bully, and incidents of such behavior will be diminished or eliminated completely. The fundamental approach is to deny the bully what he wants, which is to win in any way possible by humiliating or physically abusing others.

Teachers today are under more stress than ever before. They must cope with whirlwind technological change and all that it entails, with accelerated curriculum change, with conflicting demands from diverse interest groups within society, and with what seems like ever-decreasing time to accomplish ever-increasing tasks. On top of this they have to function in classrooms where each student arrives in the morning with a load of conflicts of his or her own, and where bullying, put-downs, and teasing can be as common as sand at the beach. To deal with this challenge, the teacher has to set priorities, and one of the first involves reducing classroom conflict.

## Creating the Environment

A case has already been made in chapters two and three for the creation of a safe and supportive classroom environment. The classroom needs to become a refuge, an oasis of relative

safety. The teacher's role in setting out such a safe environment requires establishing rules of classroom behavior
beyond routine and mundane issues like when kids can
sharpen their pencils, when they can leave the room, and
where homework is to be handed in. Rules for interpersonal
behavior are even more important, rules such as not laughing
at the mistakes of others, not using put-downs or teasing
about things others have no control over, not teasing when it
is welcome, everyone having the right to be left alone, and
leaving someone alone when told to do so.

Establishing rules like these is one thing; enforcing them
is quite another. Remember that it's much easier to enforce
rules that are specific and observable, because it is obvious
when the rules have been breached. This is an important
concept, since nonspecific, general rules are not only difficult to enforce, but difficult for students to understand in the
first place. Examples include "Everybody must get along" or
"Everybody must be nice to one another" or "Leave others
alone." Each of these is so nebulous as to be useless and
totally ineffective in addressing interpersonal conflict in the
classroom.

Further, if setting and enforcing rules are important, it is
also critical that breaches of the rules be dealt with immediately, even if that means stopping the lesson on *Austra-
lopithecus* or interrupting the deskwork in math. Conflicts
that are not quickly resolved create additional stress between
or among those involved and also act as a distraction to
learning. Although in the first month or so of school there
will be numerous interruptions while the problems are sorted
out, expectations for resolving conflicts reinforced, and
generally acceptable resolutions achieved, the long-term
results will be positive.

As students become more familiar with the expectations
and have the chance to practice the skills, incidents of
unacceptable interpersonal behavior will diminish. Teachers
should think of each incident as a teachable moment, or as
an investment in the future behavior of the class. In the short
term, everyone may be behind in the curricular areas, but in
future months when classroom conflict has been drastically
reduced or even eliminated altogether that time should be
easily made up.

## Modeling and Mind-set

Teachers must also be keenly aware of the example they set—the model they provide. This is not at all easy for many educators. Our mind-sets sometimes cause us to view conflict as something that, though unpleasant, is irrelevant to us. Our job is to teach, not to referee. Hence, we sometimes choose to ignore what we see as petty disputes, to smother the conflicts with admonitions to be quiet or to take it outside, to offload the problem by banishing the combatants from the classroom, or to dump it squarely in the administrator's lap. We say we don't have time to deal with it.

Yet, if we want kids to resolve conflicts in a positive way, we have to model that ourselves. In addition to taking the time to discuss difficult conflict issues with our students, we have to be careful that we don't employ the same tactics as bullies. If we pull rank, then we are using our power and control. If we are impatient and intolerant of kids' opinions, then we can reasonably expect that they will be impatient and intolerant too. In many ways, we have to examine our own mind-sets, decide what kind of classroom will be most conducive to reducing or eliminating petty conflicts, and choose the behaviors that model the conduct we want the kids to emulate. As teachers, we must never underestimate the incredible influence we can have on the thinking and behavior of our students. If we advocate something, then we'd better live it.

## Responses to Bullying, Put-downs, and Unwelcome Teasing

The following responses, modified somewhat from Vancouver conflict-resolution consultant Paula Temrick, are most useful when certain preconditions have been largely met. Chief among these is that kids need to know how to be assertive without being aggressive or provocative in any way. (See pages 107-109.) Assertiveness, in turn, relies on relatively healthy levels of self-esteem (discussed extensively in chapter two). It is therefore difficult to achieve success with these responses without first helping to build the self-esteem of all students. This is why simply extracting the responses and handing them to the kids will have no lasting impact. With conflict resolution, as with life I suppose, everything is connected.

For teachers or parents to be successful at helping both the bullied and the bully, specific strategies are required. Let's suppose that a bully or put-down artist has made one of the following statements: "Hah! You failed the math test again, you stupid idiot," or "Where did you get that shirt, at the dump?", or "Can't you just shut up for once? You're always babbling."

+ **Set limits to what you'll accept.** Indicate your willingness to discuss the matter, but make it clear that you won't accept name-calling or insults. Say: "Tell me what you want without calling me names" or "I don't want to talk to you if you're going to make fun of me." Setting limits tells the other person that you are willing to talk, however, you are obviously giving no credence to the provocative part, which is the name-calling or insult.

+ **Get the other person to try to solve a problem.** This is a subtle way to diffuse the situation by asking the bully or put-down artist to help solve what he perceives to be a problem. Say: "Yeah, I did fail again. What do you think I could do to pass next time?" or "Yeah, I know I talk too much. How can I break that habit?" The other person now has a choice—to continue to make put-downs or to buy into the victim's attempt to enlist his help. What the response doesn't do is pour fuel on the fire.

+ **Agree with the bully.** But be sure not to respond to the name-calling. Say: "Yeah, I *did* fail again," or "You're right, this shirt is pretty ugly," or "Yes, I know I babble a bit." This type of response tries to take the wind out of the bully's sails. Very often the bully is speechless because he got a response he was totally unprepared for. What else can we do when someone agrees with us?

+ **Clarify the intent.** You want to find out what the bully's purpose is, whether it is simple bullying or something else. Say: "So, what is it you want from me?" or "Can you tell me why it's bothering you?" This type of response tries to compel the bully to think and respond; once you manage to divert him from the path of attack, you may avoid escalation.

- **Assert your position.** Be extra careful to use the attributes of assertiveness discussed earlier, to avoid being perceived as aggressive. Say: "I wasn't trying to annoy you," or "Well, it's an ugly shirt, but I like it," or "I was just trying to give my opinion." Don't think of this as making an excuse, but rather as giving an explanation.

- **Comment on the bully's feelings.** This approach tries to turn the tables and suggest that maybe it's him instead of you who has a problem. Say: "The fact that I'm failing math really seems to interest you," or "What is it about my shirt you don't like?", or "Does my babbling really bother you?" Again, the bully is compelled to think and respond, which is something he is not used to doing.

- **Paraphrase the bully's words.** This involves confirming what the bully has said by paraphrasing the statement, thereby forcing the bully to think about what you are saying. Say: "So you think I'm stupid for failing?", or "So you think my shirt is ugly?", or "So you think I babble too much?" These kinds of questions help clarify meaning and intent while buying time to think of another strategy to try.

- **Apologize.** This should only be done when a quick mental assessment suggests that the outcome really isn't a big deal. Say: "Oh, I'm sorry if my babbling upsets you. I'm trying to break that habit" or "Sorry if my shirt bothers you, but my mom made me wear it and I don't have any choice." Apologies are really powerful because what can you possibly say to escalate a conflict if the other person apologizes?

- **Escape, but escape assertively.** This differs from silent escape, which can easily be construed as fear. Say: "I really can't talk to you when you call me names, so I'm leaving now," or "You don't seem to want to solve this problem with me so I'm outta here, " or "I'll talk to you when you've calmed down. Bye." This approach is useful when it becomes apparent that the bully is interested in nothing more than continuing to needle you until you take the bait and respond angrily.

- **Remain completely silent.** Though difficult and somewhat unpredictable in terms of subsequent taunts from the bully, the goal here is to avoid acknowledging the taunt in any way.

Proceed as though you didn't hear it at all. This is difficult to do, but sometimes works, especially in a large group.

✦ **Use humor.** Just make sure the humor is self-effacing and not directed at the bully. Say: "I don't mind failing, it's success I can't get used to," or "Sure, I get all my clothes and half my food from the dump," or "Babble? Sure, and I also burble, bubble, and bumble, too. Wanna lesson?" This kind of response requires strong self-esteem, though many kids use self-deprecating humor for an entirely different reason. Kids with shaky self-esteem often use it so that nobody else can make fun of them first.

✦ **Attempt to empathize.** This approach tries to make the bully feel that you understand his feelings and want to help. Say: "Gee, this shirt really seems to bother you," or "I can understand that my babbling must annoy you," or "I guess sitting next to a stupid idiot must really bug you." The intent here is to throw the bully off guard; nobody else has ever commented on his feelings, and he'll need time to think about this new development.

✦ **Focus on your relationship.** Try to establish some sort of positive link or bond with the bully. Say: "We've always got along pretty well before," or "Yeah, I blew it, but I could sure use your help," or "I don't think an ugly shirt should stop us from being friends." The focus is on relationship building, which will sometimes work if the bully has few friends.

✦ **Change the subject.** This tactic is not as useful as a response to the bully's comment, but is more effective when the bully becomes more persistent and after several diffusing strategies have been tried. Say: "So, you wanna play baseball?", or "So when *is* the next math test, anyway?", or "Speaking of shirts, did you see the one the principal is wearing today?" Done subtly enough, changing the subject often succeeds by diverting the bully's attention to something else he has observed or experienced.

The usefulness of the verbal tactics outlined depends largely on the degree to which teachers' and parents' efforts to enhance self-esteem and assertiveness have been successful.

It is also crucial to understand that the statements must not be viewed in isolation from each other. Typically, when a person has been subject to verbal put-downs, responses reflect a range of possible strategies. Someone being put down could try one tactic, wait for the bully's response, use a different tactic, wait to see the impact of that response, and then try another until the goal has been achieved, which is to make the bully think, to make him understand that he is not going to get what he wants, and to de-escalate the conflict before it turns into a battle.

Similarly, these verbal tactics can only become internalized by repeated practice through simulations and role play in the classroom. Simply writing the responses on the board and asking the kids to copy them into their notebooks is not enough.

A useful way to practice is to divide the class into groups of three. Within each group, give each of the members a different role. One is to play the bully, the second the bullied, and the third the observer. The bully's job is to use whatever verbal strategies he can to cause the bullied to respond with anger or aggression. Unfortunately, most students love this role and find it relatively easy to get into that character. The role of the bullied is much more difficult; he has to use the verbal tactics that have been suggested to resist giving the bully what he wants. The observer's task is to watch the bullied and to intervene when the bullied takes the bait and responds in a way that escalates the conflict. In a typical practice session, each of the three should have the opportunity to play each role.

The teacher's task is to circulate among the groups, coach the bullied when necessary, encourage everyone to stay within the framework established by the responses, and to reinforce students who have caught on to the techniques and use them to positive effect. Be forewarned, however. At first many students will find this type of role play awkward and will want to "get the right answer." Many kids, afraid to make a mistake, will think that the responses are to be used in the order that they have been introduced. Make sure they understand that the strategies are not listed in any particular order—that two, three, or even more can be used to outthink the bully or to make *him* have to think, and to subtly co-opt control of the conflict to de-escalate and eliminate it. This will take several practice sessions, with the first few probably being somewhat less than successful.

Another way to teach the verbal strategies is to invite a member of the class to verbally attack *you*. This is admittedly risky for a couple of reasons: first, some kids will revel in the chance to "get the teacher," and second, you'll have to be willing to accept taunts that run the gamut from mildly cheeky to blatantly disrespectful. This is where the power of positive modeling is particularly effective. If you as a teacher are able to accept being verbally put-down without any visible sign that you have been angered, you will dramatically demonstrate exactly the kind of defensive posture you want the kids to adopt.

After a few sessions of guided practice, it is useful to have pairs of kids go to the head of the class and play out an attempt by one to bully the other. The bullied's job is to try his best to resist giving the bully what he wants. The remainder of the class is assigned the role of observers, with the task of watching to see if the bullied falters. The resulting role plays are then used as a springboard to discuss key concepts such as self-esteem, personal power, de-escalation, win-win scenarios, peer pressure, and any other concepts that arise from the role play. None of this will work without the clearly communicated assumption of safety and trust within the class. Teachers need to work especially hard to develop an atmosphere in which kids feel secure enough to take risks without fear of reprisal. A difficult task, but essential to the success of the exercise.

Apart from time specifically set aside to teach and practice tactics for responding to bullies and put-downs, teachers need to take advantage of teachable moments in the classroom. When an opportunity to point out, analyze, and correct an act of putting down or bullying another presents itself, teachers must be willing to stop whatever else is going on and use the incident as a real-life example. Again, this will result in many interruptions at first, but as the "de-escalation ethic" becomes internalized, classroom put-downs and bullying should diminish, especially if the teacher is conscientious in modeling the tactics and strategies he is trying to establish.

Strategies to help kids build self-esteem and resist negative peer influence should be interwoven with strategies to help kids respond assertively to put-downs, bullying, and unwelcome teasing. If the teacher is both consistent and persistent in addressing these goals, the result should be a safer, more secure classroom environment, one more conducive to learning and to risk taking. By removing real or perceived threats to personal security, both teaching and learning become easier to accomplish.

## How Can Parents Help?

Assuming that bullying, put-downs, and unwelcome teasing are not permitted at home, parents' experiences with these thorns in their kids' flesh are quite different from the ones faced by teachers. This is because the perpetrators of such treatment exist outside of the parents' sphere of immediate control. A bully, put-down artist, or malicious teaser is always somebody else's kid. This presents real difficulties for a parent of a bullied child. This parent has no authority whatsoever over the other child, so efforts to change his behavior are largely useless, if not impossible. Contacting the other parent is occasionally effective, but only rarely. Most often, such complaints only serve to create a tension that has the potential of worsening the bullying instead of stopping it.

The only thing that parents can do is to focus on helping their own children respond to bullies, put-downs, and teasing with assertiveness instead of aggressiveness using the same tactics as those employed by the teacher in the classroom. (See pages 107-109.) The parents' goals are to increase self-esteem and equip their children to resist peer influence and giving the bully what he wants. In short, if parents can't change the bully's behavior, they can at least try to ensure that their own children have the tools to defend themselves.

# Removing the Thorns

If we accept that we may be faced with bullying, put-downs, and teasing all of our lives, then we have two basic options: the first, to meet the bully on his own turf and slug it out, either literally or figuratively, and the second, to adopt a position that says we will not allow ourselves to be bullied, and we will use whatever tools are necessary to resist playing the bully's game. The former approach gives the bully what he wants, which is tacit permission to administer his own particular brand of discipline. The second denies the bully what he wants and does so in an assertive, non-provocative way—a difficult task requiring careful instruction and practice, but certainly within the realm of the possible.

For whatever else they are, bullies are essentially unhappy people seeking either to feel better by making others feel worse or to drag everyone else down to their level. The moment we buy into their tactics, the bullies win the battle, and we open ourselves up to additional bullying. The best way to help the bully is by providing opportunities for him to experience positive success and then reinforcing him for it. A second method is to try to develop empathy and tolerance in the bully so that he can see the negative impact of his bullying. Raising the bully's self-esteem by means other than putting or dragging others down will be far more beneficial than the simple application of punitive sanctions.

At the same time we must work with the rest of the students, the victims of the bullies, put-down artists, and teasers. We should help these kids understand the roots and impacts of these actions and teach them useful strategies for dealing with them so that they can deflect the barbs and taunts without playing the escalation game. If all goes well, the result will be a classroom environment where the bully has nobody to bully because nobody will take the bait, and where everyone, bully and bullied alike, experiences enhanced self-esteem through success, an emotionally safer learning environment, and the lasting security that comes from the confident expectation of being able to resist bullies, put-downs, and unwelcome teasing.

To achieve such noble and lofty goals requires sustained effort, willingness to suffer inevitable setbacks, an enduring patience, and incredible persistence—all in all, precisely the same attributes required of every teacher and every parent in these difficult, conflict-laden times. While it won't be easy, it is critically important to try. Otherwise, the problems will only grow larger, and teaching, learning, and raising children will become even tougher than it already is. If we choose to make the commitment to curb bullying, then we'd better make sure we are willing to be in for the long haul. In the end, there's really no other choice.

# 5

# Building the Perfect Beast: Putting It All Together

## About Ronny

*Ronny showed up on the first day of school a couple of years ago, a sullen, somewhat defensive twelve-year-old from a small town in Manitoba. He peered suspiciously at me from under a mass of unkempt red hair and I could see he'd once had surgery to correct a harelip. As I talked to him and welcomed him to the school, I couldn't help but notice that both his fists were clenched and his responses consisted mostly of monosyllabic grunts. He'd been sent to B.C. to live with an aunt in the hope that a fresh start might somehow help him. Although I wanted to help him, his teacher wanted to help him, as did his aunt, as far as we could see, none of his classmates seemed interested in including him.*

*He soon became the butt of the kind of teasing and taunting that new kids often face. His academic skills weren't very good, and his behavior was alternately mischievous and defiant. He attempted to win friends by acting goofy, performing acts that, instead of producing a laughing, appreciative audience, resulted instead in further ridicule. The other kids were not laughing with him, but at him. When Ronny realized what was happening, he would do one of three things: start a physical confrontation with the closest classmate, hurl strings of foul language at anyone within earshot, or pack up his belongings and leave, angrily defying the teacher's attempts to calm him down enough to stay.*

*Sometime in the third week of September I spent the better part of an hour in the vacant lot across the road from the school where I'd caught up to Ronny. He'd blown up over something, and his teacher was so frightened by his outburst that she didn't try to stop him. His rage was palpable as he told me that he hated this f___ing school and all the people were a bunch of assholes, especially that bitch teacher of his—and on and on and on. He wasn't so much screaming at me as he was screaming at the world, and at that moment I saw him not as a discipline problem, but as a desperately unhappy boy who had hoped for a new beginning, but had found only the same sad, familiar story.*

*I ignored the screaming. I ignored the swearing. I can't really remember all that I said to him, but the words weren't as important as the message I tried to convey through calm persuasion. I acknowledged that he was hurting, that it was really tough to move to another school, let alone another province, and I empathized with him for having to try to fit in with a group of grade-seven kids who had been together for years and weren't too receptive to newcomers. (As a group, grade-seven kids rarely are.) I told him to tell us when he needed help or protection. And I promised him that things would get better, but that HE'D have to try harder, too.*

*It took what seemed like forever to calm him down, but finally we walked back to the school together and he returned to his class. Nobody dared say a word to him.*

*For a week or so, everything seemed fine. Ronny seemed calmer and, apart from a few minor blowups, seemed to be making progress. We kept a close watch on him and saw him beginning to play with a couple of other boys at recess and lunch. We were cautiously optimistic, but our optimism proved to be misplaced.*

*In early October, Ronny's aunt told us that he'd returned to Manitoba over the weekend. He'd caused so much disruption in his aunt's household that her own children were ready to strangle him. Within days the classroom returned to relative normal, as did the aunt's family. I thought that was the last I'd hear about Ronny, but this was not to be.*

*Just a few months ago, I spoke with his aunt. She broke down in tears when she told me about Ronny. One Friday his parents had gone away for the weekend and his older brother had left to meet some friends. With everyone out of the house, Ronny loaded the gun that had been left to him by his late grandfather and shot himself. He was only fourteen. No one knows for certain why he did it. The most that I can say is that Ronny's death was probably the result of a multitude of factors that became so overwhelming that he chose what he believed was his only option.*

There are lessons to be learned from the tragedy of Ronny's short, unhappy life. From my brief acquaintance with him I am able to make some observations:

❖ Ronny had very little self-esteem. Perhaps he was self-conscious about his scarred lip, his comparatively low academic ability, his inability to form friendships, and the negative reactions to his behavior from his peers. From what I saw, his low self-esteem was constantly fueled by the generally unkind treatment he received from his classmates. His typical reaction was based in rage.

❖ Ronny couldn't manage his anger. His propensity for screaming and swearing, slamming books and furniture, and engaging in fistfights showed that he had no concept of resolving conflicts in any other way than violence. Such violence is socially unacceptable and almost always results in unpleasant consequences. And children often cannot make the connection between the act and the consequence; they view sanctions as punishments, reinforcing their negative view of themselves. Sort of "if I did something wrong, I must be a bad person."

❖ Ronny hated not fitting in. Every human being has a need for acceptance, and we are understandably upset if we are not accepted. We adults tend to be subtle about excluding those who don't fit our criteria for friends or acquaintances; children are not at all subtle.

❖ Ronny was teased and taunted about things over which he had no control. His lip was scarred and his nasal speech sounded funny to other kids. The kind of teasing he experienced often leads to feelings of frustration and powerlessness. Ronny used fighting, swearing, and escape as ways to gain some sort of control.

✧ Ronny displayed a distinct mistrust of authority figures such as teachers and principals. This was perhaps a result of prior experience within a school system that demanded compliance. So our offers of help were not accepted, perhaps adding to Ronny's feelings of isolation and alienation.

Altogether, the image of Ronny that emerges is disturbing. He was a deeply unhappy boy; isolated, alienated, and suffering from low self-esteem. Frustration, powerlessness, mistrust, inability to manage anger, a lack of impulse control, and minimal acceptance from his peers likely played parts in the tragedy of his final decision. Even more tragic is that Ronny is only one teenage suicide among far too many. Clearly, parents, teachers, counselors, and all who are in daily contact with children desperately need to find ways to reach the Ronnies of the world

It isn't only kids like Ronny who need to learn better ways of resolving their conflicts. All children must be given the opportunity to learn strategies for dealing with complicated relationships. It's a big job, but as teachers, administrators, and parents we can and must try to make a difference.

This final chapter is designed to synthesize all that has gone before it. It is an attempt to draw together the concepts, skills, and thought processes required to raise children who are healthy and happy and capable of dealing with the multitude of complex and confusing social relationships they will face throughout their lives.

## Living with Perpetual Change

Apart from other causes of conflict—competition for scarce resources, the difference between what is and what is desired, an imbalance of power—change itself contributes to and exacerbates conflict. Changing social and cultural values rob us of our feelings of security and certainty as we struggle to make sense of a confusing and sometimes senseless world. And if change is bewildering and frustrating to us as adults, imagine what it must be like for children, who typically take their cues from the important adults in their lives.

There is little doubt that the pace and volume of societal changes are a source of conflict. Some of these are:

+ **Opposing value systems.** Children today are faced with a bewildering array of values. These varying values, which reflect an often confused and fragmented society, frequently contain the seeds of conflict.

+ **Changes in family structures.** The traditional nuclear family, with a mom, a dad, and kids living together in a single family dwelling, is no longer the social norm. More kids come from single-parent and other family configurations than ever before, creating a diversity in the classroom which, too, can generate conflict.

+ **Decreased family time.** Instead of the twenty-five-hour work weeks we were promised would result from automation, people are working longer hours than ever. The result is less time for many families to spend together, and less time for kids to learn essential life skills and lessons from their parents.

+ **Diminishing resources.** Today it seems that there is less of everything—jobs; spots in colleges, universities, and technical schools; and opportunities in general. These factors create stress in families that affect every member and often spill over into the school.

Taken together, these issues are only a few of those that contribute to an increasingly complex culture. Changes within the school system reflect changes within society. And, in the past forty to fifty years, there have been substantial changes in the classroom.

## Changes in the Classroom

At one time, the teacher was very much the boss and kids were very much subject to their authority. Kids were expected to be obedient and to respect authority. The classroom was controlled and the teacher was the controller. This type of approach was predominant until the early 1960s, when massive social changes began to take place.

In the 1960s, younger teachers began to challenge tradition, with dramatic implications for the classroom. Questioning authority became almost obligatory, and the popular approach was to liberate the students—to allow them freedom to explore their creative urges. Many teachers gleefully took on the role of liberator.

In recent years, many teachers—often those who were once liberators—have embraced the wisdom of enabling kids. Briefly, the enabling teacher both accepts and provides structure—for learning, for behavioral standards, and for consequences. Enablers provide enough flexibility to allow kids to explore their interests and to express their ideas in a variety of ways.

Essentially, the enabler picks and chooses the best attributes of the controller and the liberator and attempts to achieve a middle ground. Properly done, the result is the type of classroom that provides the best chance for kids to learn and grow in a safe, supportive environment.

## Dealing with Conflict

To deal with conflict acceptably, we must first understand where it comes from. And once we achieve an understanding of the "mechanics" of conflict, we can then begin to develop an approach to resolving conflict that is based on both a knowledge of cause and an inventory of strategies, techniques, tactics—whatever we'd like to call them—that will help us both to survive and to flourish without adding to conflict.

While it is inevitable that interpersonal conflict will occur throughout our lives and the lives of our children, it is possible to turn the tide of conflict. Such a turning requires creating a vision of the possible and then relentlessly adhering to it.

Another way of thinking about the idea of vision is to call it mind-set, as described in chapter two on self-esteem. Mind-set, with respect to helping kids deal with conflict, is the sum total of our beliefs and values about how children grow, learn, and develop into decent adults. The vision I am proposing, for both teachers and parents, has the following attributes.

## Kids with Healthy Self-esteem

It is now indisputable that healthy self-esteem is a fundamental precondition to successful learning. If a child believes he is stupid or incapable or unaccepted, he will not feel confident enough to take the risks that learning often demands. He will retreat into the safety of silent, and often morose, anonymity. This, in turn, will contribute to a downward spiral of negative self-esteem, thereby making opportunities for success as scarce as wings on a frog.

The fundamental basis for self-esteem is twofold: first, the student must experience success and be reinforced for it; and second, the student must internalize the feeling of success. Merely being told how good he is means nothing if he doesn't want to believe it. So, how do you ensure the child will internalize your reinforcement? A difficult question, but think of it as an additive process. Constant repeated reinforcement for any and all successes, no matter how trivial they appear to be, should have the effect of demonstrating to the child that he is capable in a whole variety of areas that he may simply have taken for granted.

This does not mean that you must praise everything except those things he does not do well or out-and-out fails at. If we focus on only the positives and ignore the negatives, we are sending a message that, though well-intentioned, can easily backfire. Kids need to know when they have made a serious error, but the way in which we adults deal with it has to focus on the act, not the kid.

When we praise a child, we have to be careful to praise the act or the product. The same is true when we must inevitably apply consequences for some transgression of the rules. Nothing to me is more heartbreaking than when a seven-year-old tells me, "I'm a bad boy," because he has been programmed to believe that if he does something bad, then he *must* be bad. If anyone, child or adult, constantly hears the message that he is bad, then he will not only believe it, but will eventually use it as an excuse for his behavior and as a reason for making decisions that result in antisocial or even criminal activity. Sort of "give me the name and I'll play the game."

In short, we can help build our children's self-esteem by encouraging and praising their efforts and results, by empathizing with the difficult interpersonal problems they regularly face, by allowing for mistakes and failures, by providing fair treatment, and by providing as many opportunities for success as we can find. These must take place within an environment that is safe, where children feel accepted and that they belong. Top it all off with positive role modeling and the conditions for an environment where self-esteem has a good chance of flourishing are created. To further enhance such conditions, specific skills can be taught, modeled, and reinforced. These skills include:

✦ **Assertiveness skills.** Assertiveness skills are a means of stating one's position clearly and without any hint of the type of aggression that can escalate the conflict. Assertiveness skills are extremely difficult for students to master, since so much conflict in schools emerges from verbal put-downs and the ability to come up with a quick, devastating retort is so admired by students. It's hard to be assertive when everyone else seems to be aggressive.

Assertiveness skills require much practice in simulated situations in the classroom, though the simulations can be-come a little tedious after a while. It is also difficult for students to make the transfer from classroom to real-life situations as they occur in and around the school and community. Nevertheless, practice does help if some variety is introduced in the simulated situations. (Pages 107-109 in chapter four provides a more extensive discussion of assertiveness.)

✦ **Personal problem-solving and decision-making skills.** When kids crash and burn in the first year or two of high school, it is nearly always a combination of factors related directly to bad decision making. Examples include decisions made about friends, activities, and whether or not to do homework. Those kids who do not crash are often those who are familiar with decision-making processes and usually make decisions that will turn out in their favor. Similarly, poor problem-solving skills, which are closely associated with decision making, contribute to lack of success. There are many problem-solving and decision-making models available in commercially produced conflict resolution programs, and they also exist in curriculum guides.

Helping kids develop strong problem-solving and decision-making skills is crucial to their future success, both as students and as citizens. Success in problem solving and decision making will add to their inventory of successes and will provide one more element in building their self-esteem, their confidence in their abilities to tackle difficult issues, and their ability to become independent thinkers. All in all, another piece of the puzzle of raising and teaching kids.

If we do only one more thing for our children beyond providing them with the basics of food, shelter, clothing, and so on, we should help them achieve generally healthy levels of self-esteem. Without a strong, well-developed sense of self, of capability, of acceptance, of belonging, and of physical and emotional safety, our children will be ill-prepared to function effectively in the real world.

Healthy self-esteem is the essential building block of success, and, as parents and teachers, we can improve kids' chances of developing high self-esteem by adopting a mindset that sees kids as capable of success, by modeling the behaviors and attitudes we want them to accept, and by using methods that are humane and supportive. If we can achieve these goals, our kids will be better prepared to hurdle the next great barrier: peer pressure.

## Kids Who Can Resist Negative Peer Pressure

It is axiomatic that the lower the child's self-esteem, the greater his susceptibility to peer pressure—and vice versa. Thus healthy levels of self-esteem will frequently help kids resist negative peer influence. Still, almost all pre- and early adolescents will occasionally fall under the negative influence of peers, and though we have tried to help them avoid it, we are still bewildered as to why they will apparently knuckle under to what we see as peer pressure.

Essentially, most adolescents live with the great paradox of adolescence, which is: *Let me be an individual, but please don't let me stand out from the others.* The reason for this attitude is that the social sanctions for kids who do not conform with their peers can be exceedingly uncomfortable and sometimes physically threatening. So, instead of chastising kids for not having the courage to stand up to peer pressure, understand when a child says that it's sometimes easier to go with the herd. As an adult, your patience may sometimes be sorely tested, but try to be as empathetic as possible by recalling your own experiences at that age, which were probably very similar.

Our kids are faced with three types of peer pressure: (1) overt pressure to do something they shouldn't, such as drugs, alcohol, tobacco, sex, or vandalism; (2) covert pressure, which is based on the kid's own assumptions and beliefs about how to think and behave; and (3) silent consent, which is the pressure to remain silent about all manner of crimes and misdemeanors. While each is discussed in detail in chapter three, a brief recap may be helpful.

Overt peer pressure is less difficult to deal with since it is out in the open and its products are, for the most part, easily observable. From a young age, kids can be prepared to anticipate these issues, and the chances they'll avoid them can be increased through open communication and by building up their self-esteem. Threats and fear tactics will rarely work. For example, telling a child that marijuana will lead to a life of heroin addiction on the streets of some large city will not wash when so many teens know that this simply isn't true.

Covert peer pressure is more difficult to deal with since it deals with assumptions and beliefs that kids develop by observing the attitudes and behaviors of their peers. It is sort of a mind-reading exercise that kids use to try to figure out who they are and how they fit in. If your sixteen-year-old son arrives home with a tattoo and an earring, don't necessarily interpret it as an act of defiant rebellion against your values. It may simply be his attempt to achieve a more comfortable fit with his peers. Of course, that doesn't necessarily make it acceptable to you if the issues of tattoos and earrings have been discussed and form part of your own bottom-line expectations. An act of defiance is an act of defiance, so be ready with appropriate consequences that the kid knows will be applied.

What is important is to keep talking and keep listening. Allow your kids to rebel in safe areas such as deciding which clothes they will wear, assuming that such clothing is "decent." Remember the message of Barbara Coloroso: If it isn't illegal, immoral, or life-threatening, let them do it. Sooner or later, your kids will almost certainly come to their own realization that what they thought was important to think and do was probably not. Remember that if you've taught them from a reasonable mind-set, provided strong modeling, and used open and humane methods of communication and instruction, your kids will eventually turn out fine; it's just those intervening years that will compel you to question your sanity on a daily basis.

Silent consent peer pressure is scary because it persuades kids to remain silent in the face of sometimes unspeakable cruelties committed by others. But there is often a legitimate reason for doing so, and that is fear of repercussion. Still, kids have to be brought to the point of understanding that there is always *someone* they can tell, which is why I always advise my own students to identify at least one adult in their lives who they can trust with important information. It may be a parent, a teacher, a counselor, an aunt or uncle, a grandparent, a neighbor—even a principal or vice-principal. Kids have to know that their anonymity can be assured if they are "doing the right thing" by telling.

It is unfortunate but inevitable that peer pressure and the anxieties of puberty coincide—as if kids didn't have enough to cope with as their bodies begin pumping hormones through their systems. Nevertheless, parents and teachers can help by "keeping cool," maintaining their sense of humor, and being available to talk, to listen, and sometimes to dry the tears. If parents and teachers do everything they reasonably can to help kids through adolescence, the kids should emerge from those difficult years with fewer, less visible scars than if they hadn't.

## Kids Who Can Cope with Bullying, Put-downs, and Unwelcome Teasing

Constant exposure to bullying, put-downs, and unwelcome teasing can become both tedious and mind-numbing, and the emotional scars can be deep and permanent. As teachers and parents, we can address these difficult problems by ridding our own behavior of put-downs and unwelcome teasing and by helping children to learn and use the strategies required to resist being assailed by those who try to grind them down.

In addition to assertiveness skills and the fostering of strong self-esteem, kids need time to master the verbal strategies detailed on pages 119-121 in chapter four, remembering always that *if you give a bully what he wants, the bully wins.* If I had my way, all kids would repeat that statement fifty times a day before they leave home in the morning; it is critical to their emotional, and sometimes physical, survival.

At the same time, there has to be at least a little empathy for the bullies and put-down artists; they can't simply be ignored. Teachers and parents should not only help the bullied to resist bullying successfully, they should also work with the bullies themselves to help them modify their behavior. If we recall that most, if not all, bullies suffer from low self-esteem, we can help them by employing esteem-building strategies.

Put-downs, as has been mentioned, are especially difficult to deal with. Everywhere we look in our popular culture, the quick rejoinder or the ultimate put-down is evident. We see youngsters on television sitcoms cheekily putting down adults to the approving roar of the audience, we see it in movies where conflict is the foundation of all dramas and action movies, and we see and hear it daily in and around the school as kids try out the latest insult or put-down they've heard somewhere else. Great value is placed by many kids on the ability to put the other person down with a few carefully constructed witticisms (and some *are* truly witty). Too often, though, verbal duels end up escalating into more serious conflicts, especially when someone runs out of something witty to say and relies on out-and-out insults or, worse, fistfights.

Teachers and parents must not only eliminate put-downs from their own daily practice, but must pull rank if necessary in telling their kids that, no, we don't do that here. Try to draw a connection between how put-downs from others feel and how put-downs directed toward others must feel to them. A child's response to this might be: Since others don't care about *my* feelings, why should I care about theirs? A difficult question, since the answer won't make much sense to a lot of kids. The answer is this: We have no control over how others behave, but we *can* control our own behavior. It is our responsibility to treat others the way we want to be treated ourselves. And if that sounds a lot like the golden rule, that's exactly what it is.

As far as teasing goes, kids need to understand that there is both welcome and unwelcome teasing, and that if the person being teased becomes angry, upset, or violent, then the teasing is unacceptable. The most useful guideline with teasing, is that it is only really acceptable from someone who is a close friend or a loved one, because we know they mean no malice. With strangers or even acquaintances, we are less likely to accept the same teasing since we may believe that it is intended to insult or hurt. Therefore, kids need to be shown that teasing can be just as provocative and can cause the same results as a punch in the face or a kick in the kneecap.

Needless to say, healthy levels of self-esteem and the ability to resist peer pressure will greatly help a child learn to resist bullying, put-downs, and teasing. As teachers and parents we have to do our utmost to provide kids with strong, healthy understandings about how to deal with people, as well as the skills, abilities, and attitudes that will help them succeed. Someone once wrote that "there are two things we should give our children: one of them is roots and the other is wings." In a very real sense, that is what helping kids deal with conflict is all about.

## Kids Who Can React Appropriately to Conflict

Kids need to understand the concept of fight-freeze-flee, and that dealing with conflict effectively requires first the ability to recognize these impulsive responses, and second the ability to get past them and instead think about how to respond. This is where assertiveness knowledge and skills will help.

Conflict, as we have seen, is inevitable and takes many forms. In itself, conflict is not an intrinsically bad thing, the trouble comes when it escalates or becomes increasingly more difficult to resolve without resorting to extraordinary means. Our expectations about the outcomes of conflict play a huge part in how we navigate through it. There are three possible outcomes: a win-win result, a win-lose result, or a lose-lose result.

A win-win outcome is the ideal, but like most ideals it is the most difficult to achieve. Win-win outcomes rely on the willingness of the contending parties to surrender a little to get most of what they want. Win-win outcomes are especially difficult to achieve because many of us are taught from a very young age by the influential figures in our lives —usually our parents—that there has to be a winner and a loser in any conflict. It takes a lot of teaching and modeling to convince children that win-win outcomes are always best because everyone in a dispute ends up with something positive. Win-win outcomes are especially worthwhile in situations where we have to deal with the same people on a regular and predictable basis, such as in the home or in the classroom.

Most lose-lose outcomes, where neither party ends up with much of what they want, result from a committed attempt by both participants to defeat the other. As few people willingly accept defeat as final, it is almost inevitable that the one who loses will try to find ways to retaliate. A classic example would be where two kids are involved in a schoolyard fight over a football and the playground supervisor merely confiscates the ball. Neither child is happy, and the one who originally had the ball is likely to find ways of continuing the conflict to win back some of the power and control he believes he has lost.

The win-lose outcome is the most common approach to conflict resolution because it is so thoroughly ingrained in our culture. Win-lose outcomes have their place, most notably in sports and games, but win-lose situations are usually counterproductive to useful conflict resolution. Even worse, those who become accustomed to winning have problems when they eventually run up against someone who beats them. Those who always win begin to believe that might is right, that because they win all the time, their beliefs and values are somehow superior to those of others. In the end, the win-lose approach is about power, and who can exert it in the most effective ways.

Helping kids deal with conflict is about finding all the ways and means possible to help them increase their personal power and then to use that power wisely. There is almost a symbiotic relationship among three major concepts: self-esteem, personal power, and the ability to effect win-win outcomes. Healthy self-esteem elevates a child's feelings of personal power and confidence, which make him more willing and able to tackle difficult conflicts. In turn, success at resolving conflicts has a positive effect on self-esteem, thereby further increasing personal power. All in all, this upward spiral of healthy self-image, confidence, and emerging maturity help the child handle peer influence, bullying, put-downs, and unwelcome teasing.

Finally, dealing with conflict requires the ability to get past the impulsive urge to fight, freeze, or flee and allow rational thought to take over. Kids must be taught how to de-escalate conflict and to be committed to seeking win-win solutions. If self-esteem has been sufficiently strengthened and the child has developed the necessary assertiveness skills, he should be well-equipped to cope with the daily conflicts in his life. Now, if we can envision a whole school subscribing to these goals, we have a vision of the possible. Such a vision, however, largely depends on a concept I have chosen to term the "humane classroom."

## The Humane Classroom

The strength of any school does not reside solely in the principal's office. While principals can help provide general direction and create a positive school culture and climate, it is the teachers who interact with students on a daily basis who are key. It is teachers who can create and nurture the type of learning environment that is safe, where kids feel they belong, and where they are made to feel successful and accepted. In short, it is teachers who pull together all the elements of a humane classroom.

The humane teacher is one who:

+ **sees his kids as people first and students second.** Using this mind-set, the humane teacher is the one who is aware that each student is unique with a unique set of both human and academic needs.

+ **views kids from an optimistic point of view.** The teacher, in essence, looks at the glass as half-full rather than half-empty, focusing on what the child is capable of doing. This contrasts with the teacher who focuses only on errors and sees them as evidence of deficiency.

+ **includes all students.** The humane teacher, because he believes that all kids are capable of learning, sees problem children as requiring patient and compassionate nurturing.

+ **views problems as opportunities.** The humane teacher is unafraid of constant change in the school system and instead looks upon changes as opportunities to refine and add to students' existing skills and knowledge.

+ **believes relevance in curriculum is a priority.** The humane teacher not only tries to communicate to students what he is teaching, but why the learning is important to their lives.

+ **is structured but flexible.** Instead of viewing the education system as being built on a concrete slab, the humane teacher is more likely to see it as built on a trampoline. In other words, he discerns what the kids need and how best they might learn, and then adapts the curriculum and techniques to best meet their needs.

+ **is a voracious learner.** The best learners make the best teachers, and those who continually seek ways of increasing their own knowledge and honing their own skills optimize their impact in the classroom.

+ **uses conflict as an opportunity to teach.** The humane teacher doesn't bury or ignore classroom conflicts; he uses those moments to practice resolution skills and concepts. The message this teacher gives is: I care about how people in this room feel, I know you have to feel secure to learn best, and I'm willing to help.

+ **is willing to negotiate.** The humane teacher is open to the discussion of many issues, but is careful to assert what kinds of issues are nondebatable, such as kids having to do homework.

+ **is open to alternative techniques, strategies, and views.** The humane teacher knows that perfection is impossible, but seeks to be as near perfect as he can be. This teacher has an open, inquiring mind and routinely reflects on his professional practice, always seeking better ways to accomplish the same tasks.

+ **is acutely aware of the individuals in the class.** Because the humane teacher knows that kids are more than students, he endeavors to find out as much about each child's life, interests, hobbies, hopes, and fears as he can. The goal is to achieve as full an understanding of the students as possible to more completely meet their needs.

+ **makes use of outside stimuli.** The humane teacher makes use of resources outside the classroom to enrich students' understanding of the world, its conflicts, and possible solutions.

+ **encourages and celebrates risk taking.** Knowing that mistakes and errors are not evidence of failure, the humane teacher encourages kids to push themselves further in their studies.

+ **creates opportunities for success, and reinforces student successes.** Aware of the critical importance of self-esteem, the humane teacher tries to ensure that all students are recognized for their achievements.

+ **uses a flexible, situational approach to discipline.** The humane teacher strives to make classroom rules fair and easily understood. The consequences of noncompliance are made on the basis of the student's behavioral history, degree of willfulness, and degree of remorse, as well as the severity of the crime. In short, the humane teacher makes the consequence fit both the actor and the act.

+ **is not a slave of the curriculum.** While the humane teacher is acutely aware of the demands of the academic curriculum, he doesn't become obsessed with the curriculum to the exclusion of human issues. He will take the time to deal with interpersonal problems, even if it means shortening the math lesson that day.

✦ **creates a classroom environment that is both student-centered and teacher-centered.** A completely teacher-centered classroom can easily become dictatorial, a classroom in which feelings, opposing beliefs, and petty squabbles are buried. A completely student-centered classroom can become anarchic, one in which kids may feel great about themselves, but nothing of academic significance gets done. In a humane classroom, the teacher creates the framework and routines for work and interpersonal conduct and allows a broad range of alternatives within the framework.

Creating a humane classroom is essentially a matter of achieving a balance between the demands of the curriculum and the need to create a safe haven for kids. Within a fairly rigid framework of routines, expectations, and responsibilities, students are given a high degree of flexibility in how they solve problems and make decisions. They are reinforced for their successes and encouraged to take risks that result in growth in their understanding or skills.

Humane teachers are those who have adopted a view of students that sees them as capable and responsible when challenged to do their best. Along with this mind-set, humane teachers attempt to model the behaviors they are trying to transmit to their students. Such transmission takes shape in the methods these teachers employ, methods that are aimed at enabling students rather than at controlling their every move.

Creating a humane classroom is not as difficult as it may appear to some; most kindergarten teachers have been operating this way forever. Some teachers may feel that creating this type of classroom takes up too much valuable learning time, that there is so much material to cover that they just don't have the time to interrupt a lesson to deal with interpersonal conflicts, teasing, or put-downs. This type of teacher needs to examine his commitment to teaching and ask himself the key question: "Is my role simply to transmit knowledge or is it to help children learn to function with confidence and skill in a complex society?" In essence: "Do

I teach kids, or do I teach subjects?" For humane teachers, the answer is clear: they teach kids what they need to know about life in ways that put the needs of the child on equal or superior footing with the needs of the curriculum.

## A Few Words for Parents

Much of what has been said about teachers in this book is applicable to parents as well. Though parents are not involved in the formal education process to any great degree, the same kinds of interpersonal conflicts that occur in the classroom also take place in the neighborhood and at home. Further, just as there are three basic types of teacher—the controller, the liberator, and the enabler—these terms also apply to parents.

Controlling parents are very much concerned with the behavioral training of their children. Typically, controlling parents make most or all of the decisions for their kids and frequently view mistakes as bad and unacceptable. As the children of controlling parents progress through the school system, they often lack confidence in themselves and their abilities and have a difficult time making decisions and solving problems. This is because they have had little experience in making decisions that directly affect them. The most common verbal expression used by controllers is no.

Liberating parents set very few limits on their children. Just about anything goes, and freedom is the prevailing value. While the children of liberating parents can make decisions and solve problems, decisions are made most often out of pure self-interest. The flaw in the parent-as-liberator scenario is that little attention is paid to acceptable standards of group behavior or the ability to put the interests of others ahead of, or even equal to, one's own. Liberating parents, because of their disdain for bureaucratic structures such as schools, are often very vocal in their criticism of schools, especially if their children are not afforded the degree of personal freedom their parents believe they should have. The most common verbal expression used by liberators is "whatever you think [want]...."

If controllers and liberators are at the opposite ends of the spectrum, then the enabling parent represents a balance between the two. These parents are wise enough to understand that kids need to learn standards of both personal and group behavior. Kids from enabling homes can make decisions and solve problems because they've had practice. They have empathy and understanding because those values have been modeled at home. They are open to win-win conclusions and they understand the relationship between an action and its consequence. The most common verbal expression used by enablers is "What do *you* think?"

If we recall that most of children's actions, beliefs, values, and ethics are absorbed from the dominant adults in their lives, it follows that parents have the greatest influences on their children. This is especially true for the first five years of life, but somewhat less so with the introduction of other adults such as teachers, group leaders, coaches, and so on. Nevertheless, parents have an immense impact on determining what kinds of people their children will become. This book, of course, argues for the enabling of children.

It isn't easy being a parent, never has been and never will. All manner of unpleasantness is in store for our kids: negative role models and peer influence; temptations such as drugs, alcohol, tobacco, and sexual activity; and all kinds of people who may try to bully and put them down. The most we can do is help our kids achieve the highest level of personal power possible and to have the wisdom to use it well.

## Building the Perfect Beast

Helping kids deal with conflict is a full-time job; it doesn't consist of a series of discrete lessons with nothing in between. Helping kids is an entire way of life that requires a positive and optimistic mind-set, humane and empathetic role modeling, and the use of methods that enable and facilitate growth. The ultimate goal is to help kids develop personal power, thus giving them the ability to resist what is not in their best interests, to resolve conflict without resorting to violence, and to look for commonalities rather than dwell on irreconcilable differences.

Pulling together all of the concepts in this book into a meaningful synthesis isn't as difficult as it first appears. A useful place to begin is helping kids develop high levels of self-esteem. This is done through teaching and modeling assertiveness skills, problem-solving skills, and decision-making skills. Chances that these skills will be optimized can be enhanced with encouragement and praise, empathy, allowing for mistakes and failures, fair treatment, and by providing opportunities for success. The ultimate goal is to equip kids with ways of dealing with threats to their sense of well-being and security.

Creating a warm, caring environment where success can be achieved and self-esteem can be enhanced is the primary goal of both teachers and parents. Overall, kids need to feel that they are emotionally and physically safe, that they are accepted for who they are, and that they belong. If all this can be achieved, the result will be kids who can better resist negative peer influence.

Not all peer influence or pressure is bad; it just looks that way sometimes. Certainly, kids who have healthy levels of self-esteem will be less likely to fall victim to the type of peer pressure that results in potentially harmful acts. Conversely, kids with lower levels of self-esteem are at far greater risk of being adversely influenced by their peers. Therefore, it is in everyone's best interest for kids to develop high levels of self-esteem.

Healthy self-esteem will also help kids use a variety of strategies to deal effectively with bullying, put-downs, and teasing. First, kids must understand the nature of conflict and how it can escalate through the words and actions we use to respond to a threat, either real or perceived. They have to understand that the strategies of fight, freeze, or flee are ineffective and that dealing with a threat demands getting past these impulsive reactions and instead to think rationally and carefully. In short, they should understand the need to out-think their assailants. Embedded in their minds should be the words "if you give a bully what he wants, the bully wins."

If, as parents and teachers, we are successful at internalizing the concepts and skills in this book, we have a very good chance of raising and teaching kids who see conflict not as an opportunity to obliterate their opponents, but as a chance to establish better relationships using resolution skills. These skills, in turn, are based on a firm foundation of high self-esteem, optimism, empathy, and seeing others as something other than deficient. The results of our labor will be kids who are happy, adjusted, emotionally and physically secure, trustworthy, and self-assured. It won't be easy, but nothing difficult ever is.